DIANA

The Last Year

Also by Donald Spoto

NOTORIOUS: *The Life of Ingrid Bergman*

REBEL: *The Life and Legend of James Dean*

THE DECLINE AND FALL OF THE HOUSE OF WINDSOR

A PASSION FOR LIFE: *The Biography of Elizabeth Taylor*

MARILYN MONROE: *The Biography*

BLUE ANGEL: *The Life of Marlene Dietrich*

LAURENCE OLIVIER: *A Biography*

MADCAP: *The Life of Preston Sturges*

LENYA: *A Life*

FALLING IN LOVE AGAIN: *Marlene Dietrich* (photo essay)

THE KINDNESS OF STRANGERS: *The Life of Tennessee Williams*

THE DARK SIDE OF GENIUS: *The Life of Alfred Hitchcock*

STANLEY KRAMER: *Film Maker*

CAMERADO: *Hollywood and the American Man*

THE ART OF ALFRED HITCHCOCK

DIANA

The Last Year

by

DONALD SPOTO

Harmony Books / NEW YORK

Title page photograph: Archive Photo/Express Newspapers

Page 195 photograph: AP/Wide World Photos

Published by Harmony Books, a division of Crown Publishers, Inc., 201 East 50th Street, New York, New York 10022. Member of the Crown Publishing Group.

Random House, Inc. New York, Toronto, London, Sydney, Auckland

http://www.randomhouse.com/

HARMONY and colophon are trademarks of Crown Publishers, Inc.

Printed in the United States of America

Design by Lynne Amft

Library of Congress Cataloging-in-Publication Data

Spoto, Donald

Diana: the last year / by Donald Spoto.—1st ed.

Includes index.

1. Diana, Princess of Wales, 1961–1997.   2. Princesses—Great

Britain—Biography.   I. Title.

DA591.A45S66   1997

941.085'092—dc21

[B]   97-41929

ISBN 0-609-60318-3

10 9 8 7 6 5 4 3 2 1

First Edition

For Graham Waring, M.D.
dedicated physician and devoted friend

They knew his touch would heal,
His hand would find the pain beneath.
And so they came to find and feel
The great gift of his care.

Acknowledgments

This book had its genesis five years ago, when I began research for *The Decline and Fall of the House of Windsor,* which was published in 1995. *Diana: The Last Year* then found its unexpected final shape in light of my subject's sudden death in August 1997. At that time, I decided to restructure the book to present the life of Diana through the prism of the extraordinary events that marked the final period of her life.

In this task, I was fortunate to have the help of many good and clever people as the project neared its term.

In London, I received efficient and friendly assistance from my senior researcher, Erica Wagner, who is now the literary editor of the London *Times* and an author of significant achievement. Erica put me in touch with Suzie Gilbert and with Sean Hardy, both of whom joined the London team and helped to stockpile and synthesize vast amounts of material.

Also in London, Laurence Evans was as usual a generous and important source of material; as well, he suggested several themes for my consideration. My work in London is always leavened by the devotion of my dear friends Laurence and Mary Evans.

In America, I could do no better than to have the collaboration of my longtime researcher and editorial assistant, Greg Dietrich. In addition, my good friends were always at the ready with encouragement and pertinent questions that made me rethink certain issues. Somehow they always make the doubtful real, especially on those cloudy days when it is hard to believe that the final product will ever be realized.

A C K N O W L E D G M E N T S

By coincidence, my agent Elaine Markson had scheduled a late-summer visit to me just as I was in the final stages of the manuscript. As usual, she offered the greatest encouragement, but I am afraid I was a wretched host: after breakfast, I abandoned her for Diana and the Windsors. That she took no offense (and read pages as they came from the word processor) is further evidence of what has come to be an invaluable professional relationship and a precious friendship.

In the New York offices of Elaine Markson Literary Agency, I am supported every day by the efficient and friendly team: Geri Thoma, Elizabeth Sheinkman, Sally Wofford Girand, Sara DeNobrega, Tasha Blaine and Kai Ping Lin.

I had the fondest memories of an earlier collaboration with Shaye Areheart, executive editor at Harmony Books; some years ago, she was the editor of my book *Blue Angel: The Life of Marlene Dietrich,* at another publisher. How grateful I am that once again Shaye endorsed me and my work and gave me the benefit of her considerable skills—and her valued friendship, too.

Also at Harmony, Chip Gibson, Steve Magnuson and Leslie Meredith supported the book from day one. In other departments, I must salute Rebecca Strong (in the foreign rights department), Barbara Marks (senior publicist), and for invaluable help in a number of areas, Holly Clarfield, Dina Siciliano and Sean Yule. In the production department, I owe hearty thanks to Teresa Nicholas, Laurie Stark, Mark McCauslin, Jane Searle, Lauren Dong and John Sharp. In art and design, Whitney Cookman and Mary Schuck created the impressive jacket for this book, and Lynne Amft designed the interior.

On the dedication page is the name of a man whose skill and friendship have enriched my life more than I can say. Graham Waring, M.D., is respected by his colleagues, admired by his patients and loved by his friends. I am fortunate to be counted among those who benefit from his genius as a physician and who reckon his camaraderie as one of the great blessings of my life. His professional wisdom, constancy, humor and abiding affection are among many outstanding attributes. Diana, who was quick to recognize these qualities, would also have found him a matchless friend.

D.S.
Beverly Hills
October 1997

Contents

If on life's uncertain main
   Mishap shall mar thy sail;
If faithful, wise, and brave in vain,
Woe, want, and exile thou sustain
   Beneath the fickle gale;
Waste not a sigh on fortune changed,
On thankless courts, or friends estranged,
But come where kindred worth shall smile,
To greet thee in the lonely isle.

SIR WALTER SCOTT, *The Lady of the Lake*

DIANA

The Last Year

1

TO COMFORT OTHER HEARTS

Stand still, you ever-moving spheres of Heaven,
That time may cease, and midnight never come.

—MARLOWE, *The Tragicall History of Doctor Faustus*

September 1997

For an entire week in early September 1997, London was different in every way—its usual hectic pace slowed, its mood somber, its appearance altered.

Oddly enough, statistics were mentioned frequently. But far from cold figures expressing little emotion, these numbers represented the warmest sentiments: $45,000,000 worth of flowers were sold in London and became the 10,000 tons of bouquets left at the gates of St. James's, Kensington and Buckingham Palaces. Vast throngs of citizens from all over England flocked into the West End, along with thousands from Europe and the Americas. The final estimates of visitors to London ran to three million people. Tens of thousands of mourners waited silently for as long as thirteen hours in sunshine and in rain to sign a total of forty-three black leather-bound condolence books at St. James's Palace, where the body of Diana, Princess of Wales, rested in a private chapel.

Despite the crowds, the crime rate dropped dramatically: there were a few arrests for public drunkenness, but little else to distract the police from their participation as guards of the massive mourning. All over Britain, businesses shut down, museums and shops closed. Video screens measuring 355 square feet were set up in Hyde Park, and silence fell like fog in one of the world's busiest cities as sixty million British citizens mourned as if for a family member.

On Saturday morning, September 6, the funeral march began at Kensington Palace, where Diana's body had been brought the night before. In order to accommodate the vast crowds—standing twenty deep along the streets—the distance of the march was doubled. To the astonishment of many, it was redesigned to include a route through the Wellington Arch, a passage historically reserved for the Monarch, certain members of the family and the Household Cavalry. At Buckingham Palace, the Queen and members of the Royal Family stood outside the gates to recognize the passing coffin, draped in the maroon and gold royal standard. Then the cortege continued. At St. James's Palace, Prince Charles, his sons, William and Harry, his father, Prince Philip, and Diana's brother, Charles, the Earl Spencer, all joined in, marching a few steps behind the gun carriage, which was drawn by six black horses of the Queen's Troop. The simple, elegant carriage bore its burden of the coffin, atop which were a central blanket of lilies and arrangements of roses and tulips from Diana's brother and her two sons. No one could be unmoved by the sight of the handwritten card simply inscribed "Mummy."

Members of Diana's favorite charities fell in behind—thousands of mourners, walking and on crutches, pushed in wheelchairs and leaning on the arms of friends or strangers. There were Red Cross volunteers, hospice workers, victims of land mines, people with AIDS, the homeless, addicts, orphans and their caregivers, those suffering with cancer—every condition, age and race seemed represented. It was, indeed, a procession of devotion; all along the route, spectators watched silently, tearfully.

Finally, the long cortege came to Westminster Abbey, where monarchs had been anointed and buried, and where statesmen and poets had been interred for almost a thousand years. The mourners were already in place—two thousand invited guests, led by the Queen and forty-three members of the Royal Family. Diana's mother, Frances Shand Kydd, was there with her children and grandchildren, her face a mask of stoic grief. And although the funeral was not, officially, a State occasion, there were dignitaries in abundance. Bernadette Chirac, wife of the French President, was there, along with Queen Noor of Jordan, former King Constantine of Greece, Princess Margarit of the Netherlands, all surviving British prime ministers, party leaders, senior ministers and their wives.

As they entered, the abbey echoed music by English composers (Parry, Bridge, Vaughan Williams, Elgar and Harris) and their European predecessors (Mendelssohn, Bach, Albinoni, Dvořák and Pachelbel).

Hillary Clinton led the American contingent, which included Steven Spielberg, Tom Hanks, Tom Cruise and (as if in a political afterthought) Henry Kissinger. Luciano Pavarotti and Elton John were there, along with Sting and his wife, Trudy, and Gianni Versace's brother and sister. Mohamed al-Fayed and his family took their places; they were still grieving for their son Dodi, who died with Diana and who had already been buried. Richard Attenborough, Tom Conti and a battery of English actors, artists and singers joined hundreds of the famous, the unknown and the workers from Diana's favorite charities. All stood to sing "God Save the Queen."

The coffin, borne by Welsh Guards, was placed near the high altar, and then came Charles, William and Harry, who placed wreaths of white lilies at Diana's bier.

The Dean of Westminster, the Reverend Wesley Carr, began the service by addressing the congregation, the crowds in London and the rest of the world.

"We are gathered here in Westminster Abbey to give thanks for the life of Diana, Princess of Wales; to commend her soul to almighty God, and to seek His comfort for all who mourn. We particularly pray for God's restoring peace and loving presence with her children, the Princes William and Harry, and all her family.

"Diana profoundly influenced this nation and the world. Although a princess, she was someone for whom, from afar, we dared to feel affection and by whom we were all intrigued. She kept company with kings and queens, with princes and presidents. But especially we remember her humane concerns and how she met individuals and made them feel significant. In her death, she commands the sympathy of millions.

"Whatever our beliefs and faith, let us with thanksgiving remember her life and enjoyment of it. Let us rededicate to God the work of those many charities that she supported. Let us commit ourselves anew to caring for others. And let us offer to Him and for His service our own mortality and vulnerability."

After a hymn all sang, Diana's older sister, Lady Sarah McCorquodale, stepped forward and read a selection of poetry:

If I should die and leave you here awhile,
Be not like others, sore undone,
Who keep long vigils by the silent dust and weep.
For my sake turn again to life and smile,
Nerving thy heart and trembling hand,
To do something to comfort other hearts than thine.
Complete these dear unfinished tasks of mine,
And I perchance may therein comfort you.

The BBC Singers and soprano Lynne Dawson sang a portion of the Verdi *Requiem,* and then Diana's other sister, Lady Jane Fellowes, rose to read:

Time is too slow for those who wait,
Too swift for those who fear,
Too long for those who grieve,
Too short for those who rejoice.
But for those who love, time is eternity.

A musical setting of the Twenty-third Psalm was then sung. Following this, Prime Minister Tony Blair read the famous blueprint of love from chapter thirteen of St. Paul's First Letter to the Corinthians, and Diana's friend Elton John, at a piano, sang Bernie Taupin's new words for their song "Candle in the Wind," originally composed in honor of Marilyn Monroe.

Then Diana's brother delivered a eulogy that contained loving promises to her children and, implicitly, a challenge to the House of Windsor and its tradition-bound concepts of royal decorum. It was, however, the startlingly honest and withering condemnation of the press, which had hounded his sister throughout her adult life, that would be most remarked upon in the days ahead. Several more of Diana's favorite hymns and motets were sung following Earl Spencer's remarks.

Finally, the Archbishop of Canterbury, George Carey, spoke a tribute and led a prayer.

"We give thanks to God for Diana, Princess of Wales—for her sense of joy and for the way she gave so much to so many people. . . . Her life touched us all, and we give thanks for those qualities and strengths that endeared her to us; for her vulnerability; for her radiant and vibrant personality; for her ability to communicate warmth and compassion; for her ringing laugh; and above all for her readiness to identify with those less fortunate in our nation and the world. . . .

"The Princess will be especially missed by the many charities with which she identified herself. We recall those precious images: the affectionate cuddle of children in hospital; that touch of the young man dying of AIDS; her compassion for those maimed through the evil of land mines. . . . She became a beacon of strength and a source of hope for so many."

The choristers then sang Howard Arnold Walter's words to the famous air from County Derrie (popularly known as "Danny Boy"):

> *I would be true, for there are those that trust me.*
> *I would be pure, for there are those that care.*
> *I would be strong, for there is much to suffer.*
> *I would be brave, for there is much to dare.*
> *I would be friend of all, the foe, the friendless.*
> *I would be giving, and forget the gift.*
> *I would be humble, for I know my weakness.*
> *I would look up, laugh, love and live.*

But this was, after all, a profoundly Christian ritual, and so the Archbishop proclaimed the faith as he invited everyone to prayer: "Therefore, confident in the love and mercy of God, holding a living faith in God's mighty resurrection power, we, the congregation here, those in the streets outside and the millions around the world, join one another and the hosts of heaven, as we say together, in whatever language we may choose, the prayer which Jesus taught us."

The Lord's Prayer was then recited by those in the abbey, those filling the streets and parks of London and, it may only be imagined, by countless more.

And then the Archbishop concluded: "Diana, our companion in faith and sister in Christ, we entrust you to God. Go forth from this world in the love of the Father, who created you; in the mercy of Jesus Christ, who died for you; in the power of the Holy Spirit, who strengthens you. At one with all the faithful, living and departed, may you rest in peace and rise in glory, where grief and misery are banished and light and joy evermore abide."

The coffin was lifted from its place at the high altar, borne again on the shoulders of the Welsh Guards and slowly taken from Westminster Abbey. At the west end of the church, the cortege halted.

As announced, there was at this point one minute of silence—all over Britain, from Land's End to John o' Groat's, from the dales of Northern Ireland to the windswept cliffs of Scotland, from the Channel Islands to the valleys of Wales. Men, women and children stood silently in parks, at train stations and airports, on streets and in their homes. The ten half-muffled bells of the abbey then tolled solemnly.

D I A N A

All along the road from London to Northamptonshire, there was deferential silence for a woman who—month by month in the last year of her life—shattered expectations and became a symbol of strength and courage for women the world over. At the age of thirty-six, she had just begun.

2

OF MAIDENS AND MISTRESSES

She had been forced into prudence in her youth,
she learned romance as she grew older—
the natural sequence of an unnatural beginning.

—JANE AUSTEN, *Persuasion*

July 1961— Winter 1978

When the obscure Lady Diana Spencer first came into the public arena, nothing seemed to mark her for an exceptional destiny. Wealth and connections to royal and aristocratic circles may have guaranteed a polite and comfortable life, but this could mean little more than marriage to a well-born upper-class boy. Raised to esteem dignity, breeding and decency above all, she was also maturing at a time when the pursuit of fun was almost a religious vocation.

For many of her contemporaries, this was a perilous clash, and some of them slid into trouble in the 1970s and 1980s. The availability of so-called recreational drugs, the societal freedom to enjoy casual sex, the availability of birth control and abortions, the insidious onset of lethal viruses—these, along with money and idleness, were a more dangerous combination than ever for the children of the privileged, just as disease and deprivation were the curse of the disenfranchised. For perhaps the first time in history, men and women at both ends of the economic spectrum began to suffer from the same maladies, which included both massive social confusion, spiritual chaos and the onset of an international health crisis no one could have foreseen. Frequent strikes paralyzed much of England's industrial life and London suburbs were scarred by race riots.

The Royal Family, meantime, continued to concern itself with finding suitable spouses for their heirs and arranging appropriate grouse-hunting parties.

Some things were changing, however. Marriages and divorces once considered impossible for members of what King George VI had called "The Firm" had become commonplace in the late 1970s. In 1978, for example, thirty-six-year-old Prince Michael of Kent, the Queen's cousin, wed the strikingly handsome blonde Baroness Marie-Christine von Reibnitz, a divorced Roman Catholic. That same year saw the dissolution of the marriage of the Queen's sister, Princess Margaret, then forty-eight.

Margaret and her husband, photographer and filmmaker Antony Armstrong-Jones (created Earl of Snowdon when he married Margaret), had lived apart for over two years, and now they availed of a new law that permitted automatic divorce after that interval. Tony would eventually marry a woman with whom he was then living, and Margaret was still jet-setting and nightclubbing with the doubtful Roddy Llewellyn, seventeen years her junior.

A former male model who stood tall, rode well and smiled winningly, Roddy was an amiably shiftless character whose sadomasochistic gear was not at all commonplace at the Palace. Apparently uncertain of whether he wanted a life with a woman or a man, Roddy had been more or less content for some time with a generous gentleman before he twice attempted suicide. Starstruck and emotionally muddled, he submitted to Margaret's determined ministrations.

This bizarre liaison, perhaps more than any other, shifted the categories for royal relationships. On the Caribbean island of Mustique (where Margaret owned an estate), the couple danced, played bridge and were at the center of a somewhat louche circle of partygoers. In London, too, Margaret and Roddy went about quite openly and entertained at dinners, but soon those who accompanied them began to believe that Roddy was not as enthusiastic a partner as Margaret might have wished. "I will never marry Princess Margaret," he said, adding significantly that "personal reasons would prevent it, and I have no desire to have children." No code breaker was required to divine Roddy's intent.

No one as close to the throne had cavorted so brazenly since the benighted Margaret was prevented by her own sister from marrying Peter Townsend more than twenty years earlier. He was married, and although divorce would have freed him to wed Margaret, the specter of King Edward VIII's marriage to the American divorcée Wallis Simpson still hung over Buckingham Palace. Restless, sad, constantly on the move from one social distraction to another, Margaret took Roddy through five erratic years of joint travel, occasionally interrupted by his sudden jaunts to Morocco and Turkey.

During one of his absences, some melodramatic suds were added to the soap opera. Downing a handful of unpotent barbiturates, Margaret issued a rather forlorn *cri de coeur,* felt dizzy for a while and awoke to find herself as lonely as ever and rather more hung over. Her sister and mother, meantime, hoped that each separation would mean an end of the affair. By 1978, Roddy fancied himself a pop singer and

Tony (would the horrors never end?) was, according to Margaret, "rude to me in front of the children." That was the last straw, and so the divorce was planned.

Princess Margaret Rose was the first member of the immediate Royal Family to be divorced since Henry VIII discarded Anne of Cleves. It was now impossible to consider the Windsors the guardians of a higher morality or as models of family stability. With Margaret's divorce, more and more respectable people began to question the idea of continuing the elaborate fiction of a monarchy that seemed more frivolous and less relevant with each passing year. All this was played out in the press, and no one was more attentive to the daily shifts in the habits of the Royal Family than Lady Diana Spencer. Like her namesake almost 250 years earlier, the golden-haired girl from the country paid particular attention to every character revelation that could be provided by the gossips.

Aware of the power and impact of the press—both newspapers and television—Diana developed a healthy sense of esteem for the third estate, even though she had no idea how she would handle its pressures if they were applied to her. "What are we going to do with Margaret?" the Queen was overheard to say, and her remark made the papers. A few years later, the same monarch asked, "What are we going to do with Diana?"

Charles, Prince of Wales, turned thirty in 1978 and still showed no inclination to choose a bride and produce an heir—which was now as necessary for public relations as for the insurance of the House of Windsor's future on the throne. "You've got to remember," Charles said, exploiting television to make his case to the people, "that when you marry in my position, you are going to marry somebody who per-

haps one day is going to become Queen. You've got to choose somebody very carefully."

Charles temporized, but he was no virgin. From the age of twenty
or twenty-one, he regularly enjoyed the company of a wide variety of
women round the world. Dates were under his control, of course: he
could never be asked, he always had to do the asking, and young ladies
were required to call him Sir however intimate the circumstances.

Among his most memorable romantic friendships were Georgina
Russell (daughter of the British ambassador to Spain); Bettina Lindsay
(daughter of a peer); Lord Astor's daughter Elizabeth; Lady Victoria
Percy (the Duke of Northumberland's daughter); Lady Henrietta
Fitzroy, a childhood chum; Lady Jane Grosvenor (daughter of the
immensely wealthy Duke of Westminster); Dale Harper, Lady Tryon;
and an alluring actress or two or ten. "Well, it beats the Changing of
the Guard, doesn't it?" asked Charles as he watched bare-breasted
girls dancing a fertility rite in Fiji.

In England and abroad, at sea with the navy or on land for a royal
assignment, Charles welcomed feminine attention. Maidens and mis-
tresses flirted, flattered, were awed. Most of those chosen for
repeated dates were soon stormed by reporters, and the women wearied of that sort of attention. They also wearied of Charles's diffi-
dence, for the Prince was unsure how to balance public duty (his
mother's obsession) with private pleasure (a goal his father never
abandoned). "His girlfriends never dominated his life," said Charles's
senior valet, Stephen Barry. "The only thing that dominates Prince
Charles is his work, and then his sporting activities. Girls come third.
Prince Andrew, not having the same future, can show much more
interest in girls than his elder brother ever could."

Part of Charles's dilemma, of course, was the awesome nature of
the choice he was expected to make—not indispensably based on

romance but on practical considerations. His intended had to have a good background and breeding (but not necessarily academic intelligence); she must be quite free of scandal (but was not required to be unworldly); and she had to be firmly Protestant (whether or not she was religious scarcely mattered). By the late 1970s, it was difficult to find a chaste young woman to become the baby-producing Royal Consort, a woman without much expectations who was willing to subordinate her future to that of the crown.

A small platoon of women thus came and went, among them Lady Sarah Spencer, who kept company with Charles for nine months in 1977. Poor Sarah suffered from a condition that was almost epidemic among certain young women in polite society: she was anorexic, as she admitted. "I would never have anything more on my plate than a couple of lettuce leaves. I lived on Coca-Cola and cigarettes and looked like something out of a concentration camp." This had been precipitated, she said in the openness of the day, "as a result of an intense love affair I had started, and because of other domestic upheavals concerning my family." That put the Windsors on notice straightaway that Lady Sarah was perhaps not quite suitable, since she had trumpeted her sexual experience.

When she and Charles returned from a ski holiday in 1977, she was almost proclaimed the next Princess of Wales by the press—an idea she herself firmly undermined when she told a reporter, "There is no chance of my marrying him. He is a romantic who falls in love easily. But I'm not in love with him, and I wouldn't marry anyone I didn't love, whether he was the dustman or the King of England." There was something to be said for all this modern bluntness.

Sarah's grandmother, Lady Fermoy, must have bristled when she heard this, for Lady Fermoy was a close friend and senior lady-in-waiting (with the venerable title Woman of the Bedchamber) to the

Queen Mother; both women had cherished the hope that Sarah might become Princess of Wales and the next Queen Consort. Then Lady Jane Wellesley, daughter of the Duke of Wellington, stood briefly in the spotlight with Charles and was scrutinized. Among other unpleasant habits and personal deficiencies, she did not like the Windsor sons' habit of pelting her with melon balls as if they were grains of wedding rice, and she withdrew. Anna Wallace, daughter of a wealthy landowner, was trotted out next, but when the moles at Buckingham Palace learned that she had actually lived with a former lover, she was history, as was a pretty "gel" named Davina Sheffield.

Next, Princess Marie Astrid of Luxembourg was actually announced by the press to be the royal fiancée. Zealous denials from the Palace were interpreted by the media to mean that the wedding bells were being polished and tuned. No one was more surprised than the elegant Marie Astrid to learn that she was being married off to the Prince of Wales: they had met several times, but never on romantic terms. Besides, she was Catholic, and this could create some awkwardness.

All during these years of romantic confusion, Prince Charles's most loyal attachment was with Camilla Shand. Their friendship began early in 1972, when he was twenty-three and she twenty-four.

The Shands had built more than half of Belgravia, the most fashionable residential section of London. Strong, plain and energetic, Camilla shared Charles's outdoor interests and his somewhat coarse, schoolboy humor. "She was a regular tomboy," said Broderick Munro-Wilson, a lifelong friend, "always full of beans, laughing and happy and great fun." A former boyfriend named Kevin Burke said she was "terrific fun—and sexy. She was always mentioning Alice Keppel."

The name of Alice Keppel was a running joke between Camilla and Charles. Mrs. Keppel, a direct forebear of Camilla, had been the mistress of Queen Victoria's son and heir when he was Prince of Wales and later when he became King Edward VII. Their affair was sustained with enormous dignity by Edward's wife, the great Danish beauty Alexandra, who even escorted Mrs. Keppel to the bedside of the dying King so that the lovers could whisper farewell privately. For Charles and his passionate friend Camilla, their lives seemed to mirror those of their ancestors. She was also allowed to help manage important aspects of Charles's life, and she regularly advised him about his staff, his social calendar, even his wardrobe.

What was more, Camilla was a great horse fancier. That alone made her a serious candidate for a family obsessed with the sport. "Charles lost his heart to her almost at once," wrote the Prince's authorized biographer, "[and] it seemed to him that these feelings were reciprocated." Oh, sweet circumlocution.

Time did not diminish the intensity of this bond; in fact, it always blazed at a steady level of ardor. But Camilla did not want to wait forever, and eventually (for whatever complex of reasons we may never know), she decided to accept the proposal of a career officer in the Queen's Household Cavalry named Andrew Parker Bowles; he had once courted Charles's sister, Princess Anne. They married, had two children and so briefly the relationship with Charles was interrupted. That they were lovers was readily admitted by Charles in 1994, and by 1997 he was seen openly with Camilla; indeed, he hosted a lavish fiftieth birthday party for her at Highgrove, his country house. Speaking to schoolboys not long before his marriage, Charles embarrassed his family: "I hope you infants are enjoying your infancy as much as we adults are enjoying our adultery." He was not married, but Camilla had been for five years.

Charles's hesitations about marrying Camilla (or anyone else) may have been based partly on observations of his parents. After thirty years of marriage, Elizabeth and Philip lived mostly separate lives. They had separate bedrooms, as the investigation surrounding several palace break-ins revealed, and they quarreled, sometimes loudly. "Voices are raised, acid drops," servants whispered in words that soon became a household motto of sorts as the Queen and the Duke glided to their rooms after an evening conversation.

By 1979, Charles was thirty-one and still single—hence causing his parents some anxiety. "You can't understand what it is like to have your whole life mapped out for you a year in advance," he complained. "It's so awful to be programmed. At times I get fed up with the whole idea." Objections like this did him no good, of course, for Charles could no more avoid his destiny than he could deny his heritage. One young lady after another bored him, and he became more and more depressed by the thought that his entire life was a condition of waiting for his mother to die before he assumed his real role.

Charles became more and more introspective, especially after the death of his mentor and great-uncle Lord Mountbatten in 1979. Never close to his parents, the Prince felt there was no one in whom he could confide, and so he effectively lost the capacity for that form of intimacy. His mother had always been the remote, preoccupied Queen, to whom he had to bow; his grandmother, the Queen Mother, was now eighty and hardly the best confidante for a young man; and as for Philip, "the last person Charles would have gone to for advice would have been his father," one courtier explained.

And so the Prince of Wales painted watercolors, attended family gatherings, presided at factory openings and ship christenings, planted an organic farm and supervised the renovation of Highgrove House, the 350-acre Gloucestershire estate purchased for him by Cornwall, of which he was Duke. He had settled on this site to be near Camilla Parker Bowles, who lived nearby with her new family. "You'd better get on with it, Charles," Philip told his son one day after yet another chat about the necessity of finding a bride, "or there won't be anyone left."

Half a century earlier, Charles's great-grandfather King George V changed the rules about eligible spouses for immediate members of the Royal Family. For as long as historians could determine, only other foreign royals or distant relatives were eligible to enter the closed circle, but after World War I, suitable aristocratic ladies would do very well. This concession to a dwindling pool made it possible for the Duke of York to wed Lady Elizabeth Bowes-Lyon, daughter of a Scottish earl; later, they became King George VI and Queen Elizabeth, parents of Charles's mother.

But now the list of suitable aristocrats was thinning, too. In the late 1970s, it was not easy to find suitable upper-class ladies with strong bloodlines, the stamina for royal duties, the health to bear at least two princely sons ("an heir and a spare") and, perhaps most of all, an unblemished personal reputation. There were advantages to marrying a foreign princess like Marie Astrid of Luxembourg or Caroline of Monaco, for they knew about protocol. In cases like these, of course, there was an additional problem, for the Royal Marriages Act clearly stated the unsuitability of Roman Catholics as spouses for heirs to the throne. Some parliamentary accommodation might be possible in the late twentieth century—that the children would be raised in the Church of England, for example. But that was not as easy as it sounded: this would force a mother to deny her children what ought to be one of her most precious legacies to them.

Unlike Britain's, most European royal families were increasingly less grand and royal. They did not depend on burdensome taxes to support themselves and their progeny; they held jobs; their children went to ordinary schools; they mingled easily in society; in a phrase, the royal families of Europe (Belgium, the Netherlands and Sweden, to name a few) did not imbue themselves with the mystic self-reverence that so maddeningly characterized the Windsors.

Amid all the anxiety about Charles and the unending line of wifely aspirants who were trotted out for his consideration, one candidate continued to emerge—an unlikely one at first, she then seemed more and more feasible.

Charles had been invited to a shooting party at Althorp House, Northamptonshire—the ancestral home of the Spencer family—in the autumn of 1977. The event was an opportunity to see where he was going with Lady Sarah Spencer, but it was clear to just about everyone present that things were already more than shaky. Lady Fermoy and the Queen Mother were making polite statements about attractive Spencers and handsome Windsors, while the Earl and Countess Spencer purred contentedly over their royal guests. Meanwhile, Charles and Sarah loped about awkwardly. As fate would have it, demure, sixteen-year-old Diana was there that day, speaking quietly and blushing when addressed, but otherwise almost vanishing from anyone's inspection.

Then, somehow, she was dragged into a joking match with her sisters, and Diana brightened up and held her own in such august company. "And somehow," recalled Earl Spencer, "she ended up standing at the side of Prince Charles."

Somehow, indeed. It was no accident. The girl had been almost pushed into position by the two smiling grandmothers. "That day," said Charles at the time of their engagement, "I remember thinking what a very jolly and amusing and attractive sixteen-year-old she was, and I mean great fun and bouncy and full of life and everything." When this was repeated to her years later, Diana had a keen observation: "I suppose it makes a nice little segment of history, but I think he barely noticed me at all."

When England's Queen Anne died childless at the age of forty-nine in 1714, there was some commotion about her successor. An Act of Settlement had been passed in 1701, requiring that the crown never pass to a Roman Catholic but only to the late king or queen's Protestant relatives. The news sent shock waves throughout the country for a very good reason: the next sovereign of England was a fifty-four-year-old German prince from Hanover, the great-grandson of King James I. He spoke no English and was not at all interested in British life and culture, but soon there he was—George I of England, monarch of a kingdom he never understood. From that day to this, German stock has predominated in the Royal Family.

The king died thirteen years later, in 1727, and his German son followed him onto the throne as George II. His son Frederick was soon named Prince of Wales, a title traditionally given to the King's oldest son, and both the court and the English aristocracy scoured the lists of eligible brides for the heir apparent. Sarah, the Duchess of Marlborough, who had been both intimate friend and canny manipulator of Queen Anne, now came forward with the idea that her attractive blond granddaughter, the aristocratic and wealthy Lady Diana Spencer—whom Sarah called "Di"—would make the perfect Princess of Wales. That match was never made, however, and the frail Diana died of tuberculosis at twenty-five. For almost twenty more years before her death in 1744, Sarah tried to bring a member of her Spencer family to the throne of England.

Her ambition was unrealized until 1981, when her descendant—another blond Lady Diana Spencer—married another Prince of Wales, Charles by name, the eldest son of Queen Elizabeth II. Mingled with the sturdy Teutonic lineage that had endured past the Hanoverian Georges through both Queen Victoria and her consort Prince Albert, Charles had Greek-German ancestry on his father's side and Scottish-German on his mother's. The heritage of Lady Diana, who sprang from one of England's oldest, wealthiest and most aristocratic families, included five lines of descent from Charles II. She counted earls and marchionesses, dukes and duchesses, barons and scores of mere lords and ladies among her forebears, very many of whom (Bedfords, Richmonds, Graftons and Marlboroughs) enjoyed royal patronage and prerogative. Diana was, then, wholly English, and her family had been for over a dozen generations on familiar terms with all the monarchs.

Diana's grandfather was the seventh Earl Spencer, an almost stupefyingly neat but pathologically rude man who feared none and intimidated all; for years, he practiced the quaint custom of greeting callers with a loaded shotgun. If the visitors were unwelcome or if the Earl remembered an offense, he simply lifted the firearm and at once watched the arrival turn to a departure. For all that, the old Earl fancied art and literature and was in fact a gifted museum curator.

This man's only child was Diana's father—Edward John (Johnnie) Spencer, born in 1924. Whereas the Earl was blunt, terrifying and inclined to bookishness, Johnnie grew up to be an amiable chap, a genial socialite, country gentleman and animal lover with no particular pretensions to excellence of any sort. Still, after service in World War II, his family name got him a position as an aide to the Governor General of Australia before he was invited to join the staff of George VI as equerry. After the king's death in 1952, Johnnie Spencer served the young Queen Elizabeth II as Master of the Household.

He resigned his post in 1954, at the age of thirty, when he married the elegant beauty Frances Roche, eighteen-year-old daughter of Baron and Lady Fermoy. The wedding, at Westminster Abbey, was the social event of the year, and Queen Elizabeth and Prince Philip were among the 1,700 guests. The Spencer and Roche connections to royals continued apace, and Johnnie and Frances Spencer, called Viscount and Viscountess Althorp, at once began a family. Sarah was born in 1955 and Jane in 1957; in January 1960, an infant son died a few hours after birth.

Diana Spencer was born on Saturday, July 1, 1961, at Park House, built near the royal Sandringham estate to accommodate the staff of Queen Victoria's eldest son—the Prince of Wales, later King Edward VII. A son and heir to the earldom at last arrived in 1964; he was named Charles. "She was a delightful child," said Diana's father, "and as a baby she could have won any beauty competition." This kind of opinion, of course, is not uncommon among parents, but hundreds of photos support Johnnie Spencer's pride.

While tensions mounted in central Europe and throughout southeast Asia, and while America endured the tragedy of President

Kennedy's assassination, Diana's childhood seems, in retrospect, almost hermetically sealed from the rest of the world. The safety and security of Sandringham, occasional visits from one or another member of the Royal Family (Prince Andrew was a year older than Diana, Prince Edward three years younger), the quiet gentility of Gertrude Allen, the old family governess—much of Diana's early history sounds like something out of a cozy, nineteenth-century children's book.

Until she was six, Diana in a sense knew neither deprivation nor unpleasantness, neither shock nor denial of any prerogative. But in another sense her early years were "hell," as her friend Peter Janson has said. "Her parents hated and despised each other by this time. She grew up in that kind of atmosphere."

There was a refuge of sorts, however. The Spencer clan always remembered the girl's fondness for small animals—not only kittens and puppies, but guinea pigs, gerbils and chipmunks. By the time she was three, she was even volunteering to take care of visiting infants. "She loved soft toys," according to Johnnie Spencer, "but she loved babies more." As a teenager, Harry Herbert (later manager of the Queen's stables) socialized with Diana and her siblings. "She always had this incredible concern for others and was the first one around if someone went down with flu. I remember, when she was sixteen, she cooked up some soup and brought it to my brother." The atmosphere at Park House, icily polite, left her to find and generate affection where she could.

Shy and in awe of her older sisters (who were ten and eight when she was four), Diana learned the proper manners her mother inculcated and the politenesses expected of a well-born young country girl. Long before she was off to school, her family had nicknamed her "Duchess." It was this timid, pretty little rosebud that Prince Charles first glimpsed on an afternoon visit to Park House when he was sixteen and Diana was three; neither of them took any interest in the other.

Diana may have been adorable, but the child was no saccharine storybook heroine. Told by her nanny that she ought to finish a portion of vegetables or the crusts encircling her bread, she smiled and nodded obediently—but a moment later she deftly stowed the unwanted morsel in a cupboard or desk drawer. She was a child alert to her own best self-interests, which was much the way her parents raised the four young Spencers.

Life with the Spencers must have seemed idyllic to most outsiders, but there was a blight in the core of its being. By late 1966, when Diana was five, her mother grew monumentally bored with the rustic life and weary of Johnnie's narrow range of interests—local committees, animal husbandry, hunting and country gatherings with her gruff father-in-law. Nor was Frances cheered by the thought that the Earl's ultimate demise would put her and her family in the ancestral estate, the baronial Althorp. Instead, the Viscountess, a sophisticated woman who loved theater, good music, witty conversation and London nightlife, decided to spend more time in town.

Perhaps it was inevitable, for from the beginning more separated than united Frances and Johnnie. As it happened, she soon met Peter Shand Kydd, heir to a paint and wallpaper fortune, and—very discreetly at first, then with less concern for public opinion—they became lovers. A suave ex-navy man, Shand Kydd was eleven years older than Frances; he, too, had a spouse and children. Never mind: in the spring of 1967, Frances simply left Park House and her family.

"One day, she was just not there anymore," according to one of her servants. Peter Shand Kydd acted similarly, and in no time the lovers—for the moment blissfully free of any responsibility—took a flat near Cadogan Square, Chelsea. The rebellious spirit and quick pace of the late 1960s were having an effect upon even the politest families in England. For some independent aristocrats as for many disaffected students worldwide, Carnaby Street seemed more exciting than Savile Row, the Beatles drew more attention than venerable church choirs, and the Age of Aquarius was dawning. For the moment, it all seemed like so much fun.

Inevitably, people were hurt. At first, Johnnie was surprised to be abandoned; soon, however, he recognized that his marriage (apparently like Peter Shand Kydd's) had really been a formality for several years. The two older Spencer girls, now ten and twelve and enrolled in boarding school, wept loudly as they shuttled back and forth for visits to their parents on alternate weekends. All the old certitudes and securities were forthwith ruptured—for those who were reading about the aristocracy at Ascot as much as for those who never missed an issue of the radical underground newsletters popular at the time.

The implications for the future were as unclear to six-year-old Diana as they were to her three-year-old brother Charles. After Christmas 1967, however, acting on advice of counsel, Johnnie Spencer announced that Diana and Charles would not be permitted further visits with their mother in London. Divorce proceedings were begun, and to her surprise Frances Roche Spencer found her own mother, now highly placed in the Queen Mother's household, testifying against her.

Even with Lady Fermoy's denunciation, Frances might have had a chance at winning at least the custody of her younger two children.

But unfortunately at the same time Mrs. Shand Kydd also sued for divorce, identifying Viscountess Spencer as an adulteress. Peter did not contest, and a divorce was granted to his wife; he lost custody of his three children. The Spencer trial, meanwhile, took a bitter year before becoming final in the spring of 1969, just before Diana turned eight. Not long after, her mother became Mrs. Peter Shand Kydd, and she and her new husband settled down—first in Suffolk, where Diana occasionally visited, then in Scotland and later still in Australia.

But this was not, as was so often reported, the end of Diana's relationship with her mother. To be sure, she was taken under the capacious wing of her grandmother, the formidable Lady Fermoy, a connection which also put her in touch with the Queen Mother. And so grew, quite naturally, the royal connection that had become the habit of her lineage. "But she was never out of her mother's sight for long, no matter where [Frances] lived," according to Peter Janson.

At first, Riddlesworth Hall in Norfolk provided distractions from the traumas of a torn family; there Diana lived, studying the usual elementary and secondary school subjects from the age of eight to just before her thirteenth birthday in 1974. She loved to dance and even hoped to make that her profession, but she grew too tall too soon and was dissuaded from her ambitions. She attracted friends, for she was a good listener and a generous classmate; and she heaped affection on a cuddly guinea pig named Peanuts, which won a prize for whatever a brilliant guinea pig can accomplish. Diana also had a cat she adored, and when it died suddenly she was heartbroken. As for riding, which was expected of girls in her social class: after falling from a pony and nursing a fractured arm for three months, she avoided the sport forever except from a safe distance. Her favorite exercise was then, as ever after, swimming, and she was always the last one out of the pool at Riddlesworth.

And then, as if on cue, the separations accumulated. Her governess, Gertrude Allen, to no one's surprise, resigned her post, because the children were away at school and there was no longer any reason for her to remain with the Spencers. Nevertheless, the news of Gertrude's departure pitched Diana into a fit of weeping. It must have seemed to her that no relationship was constant, that eventually everyone was destined to abandon her. Such a reaction might sound melodramatic to sensible older girls, but to a child who had known severe family discord and the disruption of the family nest, everything was now held suspect and Diana became a cautious girl who longed to please.

Diana's peers rarely saw her as carefree or spontaneous, and several have remarked that there was always an air of sadness about her. Accordingly, some classmates were moved to pity and they often offered her comforting little treats. Such blandishments are frequently part of the sympathetic reaction to a certain type of wistful melancholy displayed by pretty, privileged girls.

"In a way, she was a sad little kid," said a Norfolk neighbor. "Not a morose girl, but lost and certainly deprived [emotionally]. What Diana lacked and so deeply missed was a real family life. She may have been the daughter of an heir to an earldom, but any little girl with an ordinary mother, father and, if you like, a backstreet home in the East End of London was richer by far than she was in those years."

But she was not unduly self-absorbed. A certain natural empathy seemed to bind Diana to any of the younger girls at Riddlesworth Hall when they were ill or unhappy about something. "She was awfully sweet with the little ones," recalled her headmistress of the eleven-year-old Diana, who easily filled the role of gentle surrogate mother to schoolmates two or three years younger and in need of comfort, attention or help. That is not surprising, for in a way, then and later in life, Diana was offering others precisely what she herself needed. "But apart from that sweet sympathy, I can't remember her very clearly. She seemed—well, a perfectly nice, ordinary little girl."

Diana Spencer grew up as the prototypical shy English rose, and her life up to her late teens was, apart from the sad disruption in family life and the increasing distance from her mother, neither exceptional nor exciting. She was never taken to the theater, nor even to a zoo or circus, and her life lacked as much cultural stimulation as it did serious education. In her socially designated role as the daughter of venerable country gentlefolk, Diana learned to be (and so she was described by another retainer before she, too, retired) "every bit an actress, astute and devious, but nonetheless sympathetic, genuine and sensitive."

In 1975, when Diana was fourteen, her social status was altered. Her grandfather, the seventh Earl Spencer, died at the age of eighty-three, thus allowing her father finally to succeed him. He was now Edward John, the Eighth Earl Spencer—and so *his* eleven-year-old son became Charles Viscount Spencer and the girls became Lady Sarah, Lady Jane and Lady Diana.

Changes followed in every department of life, for the following year Earl Spencer married an agile, vivid woman with the colorful name Raine. She was the forty-six-year-old divorced Countess of Dartmouth, the daughter of the perpetually pink-clad novelist Barbara Cartland. "Raine had brains and beauty," said Johnnie Spencer, who was not untutored about women, "and she came to me as an older and wiser woman than many I had met."

By this time, Diana was at the West Heath School in Sevenoaks, Kent—the sort of polite, pretty place where the dormitories bore the names of flowers. Here, Diana was popular and a "normal and average" student. "She was not very sure of herself," recalled a classmate. "I remember when one of us complimented her on a cashmere suit she was wearing. Diana blushed and said, 'Mummy buys them for me.' Which Mummy we didn't know, but at that age the rest of us hated anything Mummy suggested!"

From 1976, visits home meant trips not to Park House but to the family estate called Althorp in Northamptonshire, the Spencer residence for over four hundred years. Set in 15,000 acres, the principal mansion is complemented by several additional houses for retainers and staff, as well as buildings leased to tenants. The family's quarters—a baronial mansion embellished with an art collection that includes works by (among others) Rubens, Van Dyke, Gainsborough and Reynolds—comprised something out of a vintage Hollywood movie. There were elaborate gates, a long and winding drive flanked by ancient trees, vast lawns sweeping toward stables. A comparison with Daphne du Maurier's fabled Manderley would not be farfetched.

Diana's relationship with her stepmother was predictably cool, if not downright gelid. There was no ill will, but Raine—who lost custody of her children when Lord Dartmouth charged adultery in his divorce suit—at once set herself the task of becoming the mistress of Althorp and the new Countess Spencer. Devoted to Johnnie, she understandably wanted an entirely new life for him, and by 1976, all the children were effectively out of the family nest and the redecoration and restoration of Althorp was under way. "A century of gravy has come out," said Raine, staring down at the newly resplendent carpeting in one dining room.

Barbara Cartland visited often, armed with a collection of her latest romantic novels. On holidays and weekends, Diana would seize the books, find a comfortable corner and begin reading. Pinned to her walls, at school and at home, were portraits of Charles, Prince of Wales: he would be her first guest when she was permitted to host a tea dance, Diana told her sisters.

Perhaps to that end, she became quite an agile dancer. By the age of sixteen, she was five feet seven inches tall and seemed all legs. Blond and blue-eyed, Diana blushed easily and demurely lowered her gaze when addressed. Of sex she was completely innocent, of boyfriends ignorant, and so her life remained even after a term at the exclusive Institut Alpin Videmanette in Rougemont, Switzerland. The finishing school offered casual courses in French, housewifery, dressmaking, social organization and cookery. Diana excelled most of all in skiing. "She was a lovely girl," according to one of her teachers, "but a rather young sixteen. Very idealistic, not good at French but quite serious about working with children and having a brood of her own."

But by the middle of 1978, with her seventeenth birthday approaching, Diana was ready to quit the Institut and return to Althorp. For one thing, her father had suffered a stroke and Diana needed very much to be wanted by him. As it happened, Raine was an extraordinary nurse and companion during Johnnie's recuperation after a long coma. But she also was something of a wedge between Johnnie and Diana; she kept her stepdaughter at a distance and continued to sell pieces of furniture and furnishings, regularizing the house accounts at Althorp but also in effect restructuring life there according to her own function as its sole chatelaine.

There were, however, other reasons for Diana's desire to leave Switzerland. For one thing, she was now on better terms with her mother, who had moved to Scotland and welcomed her daughters there for summers and extended holidays. And perhaps most important, during the autumn of 1977, Diana had met and been duly bedazzled by Prince Charles.

"I would love to be a dancer," Diana told a friend during a telephone call back to Switzerland. And then she giggled. "Well, I'm too tall, actually. Maybe a swimmer. Certainly a mother." And then she laughed uproariously: "Well, I can always be the Princess of Wales."

3

THE ARRANGEMENT

Have you seen a room from which faith has gone?
It is like a marriage from which love has gone,
there is patience, patience everywhere, like a fog.

—GRAHAM GREENE, *The Potting Shed*

Winter 1978—Summer 1996

From that crisp, smoky November afternoon in the countryside, Lady Fermoy and Queen Elizabeth the Queen Mother again swung into action. Charles was twenty-nine, to be sure, and time was at his heels. But he had waited this long—could he not wait another two years or so for Lady Diana to reach her maturity? Here was a right and proper girl, chaste, modest, deferential and not at all connected to the mad fashions of the day. And in the bargain, she was neither an esthete nor an intellectual, neither particularly pious nor an outright rebel. Pretty, healthy and not too gifted, she might be just right. Besides, here was a way of thwarting Lord Mountbatten's plans to deepen his family's alliance with the Sovereign: he was pushing his granddaughter Amanda Knatchbull toward Charles. The Queen Mother, who never really liked Mountbatten ("We take him with a pinch of salt"), would have none of that.

Most important of all, the shy Lady Diana could be molded according to any worthwhile plan—at first sheltered, then trained and fitted for everything the Royal Family and court tradition required. The idea of Diana as a brilliantly suitable candidate quickly caught fire between the two grandmothers that season. Thoroughly English, Diana would handily increase the English stock of the Windsors, which was a significant consideration at a time when anti-monarchist sentiment was once again rumbling around the Commonwealth. Not incidentally, she would become the first Englishwoman to marry an heir to the throne in more than three hundred years.

The Royal Family could certainly benefit from a healthy influx of English blood to counteract their own lineage. For over two centuries, since the time of the Hanoverian Georges, right through Queen Victoria and her consort, the monarchical house of England had been essentially German. The family name (and little else) had been changed from Saxe-Coburg-Gotha to Windsor at the height of World War I, but no one was fooled. The bloodlines were Teutonic, and the only dilutions of any significance were from Greece (in the case of Prince Philip's father) and from Scotland (in the case of the Queen Mother's origins). For the Prince of Wales, nothing would be better than an English bride, pure in every sense of the word.

The timing, of course, was perfect. Charles had grown disenchanted with Lady Sarah Spencer's emotional and physical problems, and he had quarreled with one or two other girls; he very much needed to console himself with an adoring admirer, and here were his grandmother and the elegant Lady Fermoy, ready with just such a one.

"In many ways it was an arranged marriage," said none other than Harold Brooks-Baker, managing director and editor of *Burke's Peerage*.

"Prince Charles needed a lovely wife, and Lady Diana fitted the bill. She was an infatuated nineteen-year-old only too eager to marry him."

As for Diana, she was a virgin and she was in love with the history of her country, incarnate before her in the most eligible man in the realm. "This is the stuff of which fairy tales are made," said the Archbishop of Canterbury on her wedding day. Referring to that romantic proclamation, Diana later said of her long courtship and marriage, "Here was a fairy story that everybody wanted to work. It was also a situation where you had to either sink or swim, and you had to learn that very fast. I swam."

This she did not only metaphorically but literally in 1978, renewing a regular round of serious physical exercise that included long daily swims whenever possible, and pitching herself into a serious weight-loss program—not because she was fat, but because (like her sister Sarah) she thought she was not as attractive as the gaunt models and superstars who were establishing an unnatural and unhealthy aspect for so many to emulate.

At sixteen, Diana could hardly be pushed at Prince Charles. Lady Fermoy and the Queen Mother, however, made it their business to see that hints were served along with the tea. In August 1980—now a slim blonde eager to grow up—she received an invitation onto the royal yacht *Britannia* for a party that included other members of the Queen's circle. "She had a charming artlessness," according to Stephen Barry—that is, she appealed by not seeming to exert any conscious appeal. "But Prince Charles's eyes followed her everywhere."

Whatever impression Diana made that summer day, it was sufficient to earn her another invitation, this time to Balmoral Castle— the Windsors' Scottish estate—the very next month. And during the following months, Diana was invited to Highgrove for a few days. On at least one occasion, Charles invited Camilla Parker Bowles to join them: he wanted her assessment of the prospective bride, and Camilla was most enthusiastic. She urged Charles to marry Diana because, according to Camilla's brother-in-law, "she thought Diana was either half-witted or mad, and thus easy for him to manipulate."

Henceforth, wherever the Prince and his new fair Lady went, the press was sure to go; for the moment, this was accepted as inevitable and even necessary (good for the image, good for the family, good for the country). The Queen, meanwhile—surely encouraged by her mother—began to see the value of Diana, whose shyness seemed to indicate submissiveness. Her inexperience was seen as a tremendous asset: she was unspoiled, with no life to be refashioned.

At the same time, the very solid differences between Charles and Diana were blithely ignored. He loved riding, which she hated; he coveted a certain bookishness, but her most serious reading was Granny Cartland's literary soaps; he liked private evenings with trusted old friends, while she wanted to see the latest restaurants and movies. For relaxation, Charles went fishing; Diana was bored by streams and heather. He loved chamber music and attempted to master the cello; her tastes ran to rock and pop, preferably the American variety.

Unfortunately—and this no one could have foreseen at the time, much less discussed—they had one major tradition in common. Neither of them actually *worked,* and their indolence denied them both the chance for a larger view of the world and a certain kind of emotional growth within it.

For her part, the Queen was repeating one of Victoria's worst miscalculations, for just as in the case of Charles's ancestor King Edward VII, he was denied any effective role. Always in the wings, forever being prepared for his full duties (but only in the most peripheral and superficial ways), the Prince of Wales was an earnest man without a very clear sense of direction. By his thirty-second birthday in November 1980, sufficient pressure had been brought to bear on him by his family that Charles realized he might as well choose Diana Spencer for his princess. Besides, this certainly did not mean he had to give up every other woman (and certainly not Camilla, for whom he always managed to find the occasional trysting time).

From the first fateful meeting in 1977, it was decided that if the Charles-and-Diana story were to move further, the girl ought to live in London—at least so that the public could become accustomed to the sight of them together. Would Diana not like to live in the capital, where society (and who knew what else) awaited her? It could be arranged by Lady Fermoy with just a word to Johnnie and Raine Spencer.

And so it was. Diana, who loved children, landed a part-time job looking after five- and six-year-olds at the Young England nursery school in Pimlico, where she identified herself as Miss Diana Spencer. "She made it very easy," said one of her coworkers, "to forget that her father was rich and an earl."

At the same time, her parents bought her a share of an apartment in a huge complex (Coleherne Court in Old Brompton Road, Earls Court), where she lived with Virginia Pitman, Carolyn Pride and Anne Bolton—a cooking student, a musician and a junior secretary. In addition to caring for the youngsters at Young England three days a week, Diana was a nanny for one-year-old Patrick Robertson, the child of American parents then living in London.

When she came to the Robertsons, the boy's mother Mary recalled, "she did not tell me she was seeing Charles." But eventually, one morning toward the end of 1980, there was a small platoon of reporters and photographers outside the Robertson house. "She said they were waiting for her, and it was because she had been at Balmoral to see Charles." According to Kay King, headmistress at Young England, "She was absolutely as happy as anyone could be. But it was dawning on her just what she was getting into. The penny was very much dropping, and it daunted her."

The press attention continued nonstop, and Diana could scarcely duck out of her apartment, rush to the nursery or attend the Robertsons without a crew of journalists at her heels, their cameras thrust virtually to her nose. And here the Palace made a dreadful mistake. Diana received no guidance from press officers on how to speak to them, how to act in public when confronted with the media. Given this lack of support, she acquitted herself with remarkable calmness and good manners; in fact, she was effectively denied the training she both required and expected in order to learn the codes of court conduct and royal protocol. She was, in other words, very much on her own. "One minute I was a nobody, the next minute I was Princess of Wales, mother, media toy, member of this family—and it was just too much for one person to handle."

It would, however, be perhaps naive to consider Diana as a lamb thrown before wolves. Certainly some members of the press were concerned only with getting the best stories, obtaining the telling photo, the astonishing remark on the record, the display of emotion that would satisfy a public endlessly ravenous for private detail.

On the other hand, Diana's shyness must not be identified with abject humility, and in this regard the media had to some extent a willing victim. She had always been in the shadow of her older sisters, always felt that perhaps she did not matter so much to the people who mattered to her. At school, she failed to qualify for university, nor did she singularize herself in any academic or cultural pursuits; she was a country girl who hated riding; she had no aptitude for music; and though well bred, she was astonishingly unworldly.

The result of this was a young woman who desperately needed to feel wanted—*validated* is one of the clichés of our time—and according to the ethos of modern life, nothing so confirms self-esteem as media attention. Diana Spencer was receiving, in other words, the attention from the press that she needed in order to feel alive and valuable. This is what she had seen on television from her childhood—people receiving the adulation of the masses—and this was perhaps the only way that the child of a broken home, the girl with two confident, strong older sisters, the adolescent with the commanding stepmother could have any sense at all that she was worthwhile. The blunt, unapologetic intrusiveness of the media frightened her, but she needed it. The paradox would dog her throughout her life and give an ironic twist to a remark of her brother, Charles: "After her childhood, she had the most bizarre life imaginable."

Much of the admiration and praise offered to Diana, in life and death, had to do with the spurious belief that she was an ordinary girl ("one of us" or "the people's Princess"), which is nonsense. Her background was privileged and rarefied, and once the royal favor fell on her she never again knew anything but a "bizarre life." To be sure, she learned and grew, and she made the role of royal princess entirely her own while conforming to no standard except that which seemed right to her.

Especially in the last year of her life, she worked doggedly to find the proper balance between service to others and to herself: with canny maturity, she never abandoned the fundamental belief that if she lost herself in the presence of others, she would have no sense of who she was or where she was going. Those "others," of course, included (perhaps preeminently) the Royal Family, and here was the point at which she began to change the way that impossibly antique institution was forced to gaze out at the rest of the world.

On February 24, 1981, Buckingham Palace announced the engagement of the Prince of Wales to Lady Diana Spencer, and the press trampled across the palace gardens to put questions to the couple and to snap photographs. On Diana's finger was a $50,000 sapphire and diamond engagement ring. Were they in love? asked a reporter of no great ingenuity.

"Of course!" said Diana, smiling.

"Whatever 'in love' means," Charles remarked. That ought to have put the girl on alert. Great romances are not ordinarily manifested with such restraint.

But this was, alas, not at all the great romance the world wanted to believe and that Diana anticipated. *She* was in love: it never occurred to her that Charles might not be. "I expect it will be the right thing in the end," he confided to a friend at the time. "I do very much want to do the right thing for this country and for my family, but I'm terrified sometimes of making a promise and then perhaps living to regret it."

He may have been thinking of Camilla Parker Bowles, still his great love. "I asked Charles if he was still in love with her," said Francis Cornish, the Prince's assistant private secretary at the time, "and he didn't give me a clear answer."

Meantime, cameras clicked and pressmen jotted notes. One warm day at Young England, Diana and her colleagues decided that the only way to dismiss the photographers was to submit to one wild profusion of snapshots, and so she stood with two children in a small garden. But the sunlight shone through her translucent skirt, and within hours the world had a view of shapely legs unencumbered by a half-slip. "I was so nervous about the whole thing," Diana said later, "that I never thought I'd be standing with the light behind me. I don't want to be remembered for not having a petticoat."

"Damn fine legs," said Charles to his senior valet, proudly tearing out the magazine photos of his fiancée. But his mother the Queen was not amused.

In 1996, the marriage of Her Royal Highness The Princess of Wales was on the verge of dissolution, and a divorce was in the works. Diana was, therefore, conferring with her attorneys about a financial settlement.

Just how much money did the Royal Family have, and to what would Charles agree? What about custody and visiting rights for their sons, who were significantly placed in the line of succession to the throne? What about perquisites: could she hope for airplanes, staff, royal residences?

And what about titles: surely, on divorce, she would retain the "Royal Highness" that carried so much cachet, especially in foreign society? "I appreciate your support and your affection," Diana had told an American reporter at the end of a recent visit. "You will be seeing a lot more of me from now on." Would she become a royal exile once her divorce was settled? Where? In East Hampton? Malibu? Rumors flew across the Atlantic like migrating wild ducks.

Royal finances were always a notoriously private matter, but this much was clear from public records. Apart from the fact that his mother the Queen was the richest woman in the world and had literally incalculable wealth stored everywhere, the Prince of Wales had an annual income of more than £5 million (about $8 million) just from taxes levied in Cornwall, of which he was Duke. That amount, and many more millions of pounds invested for him in family trust funds, was taken as a guide for the calculations of Di, as the negotiations were called. (She always hated that nickname, which was used only by those who did not know her.) The Princess's lawyers decided to seek an outright sum in the neighborhood of £50 million cash ($80 million), which is not a bad neighborhood.

But there was more to Diana's life than planning for her future: there were concerns for the present.

In June, she had gone to Chicago on a fund-raising visit to benefit cancer research. She dined and danced, and—at over five-feet-ten and wearing a shimmering blue silk sheath slit up the side to reveal long, sexy legs—she looked radiant all evening. Her schedule was not, however, merely social and glamorous. At the beleaguered Cook County Hospital, she cradled a child close to death who had most of his intestines removed, and after visiting other children ill with cancer, she sat with a man paralyzed after a gunshot battle. Then she returned to hold the hand of the dying baby she had first met an hour earlier. When she departed the hospital, Diana looked grave, and her eyes were glazed with tears.

"People ask what good such a visit can possibly do," commented Dr. William Hayden, director of Pediatric Critical Care at the hospital. "Well, I saw a lot of smiles from patients. She exudes intelligence, her questions were sharp, her eye contact real, her emotions readable and appropriate and her smile heartwarming. How much better does it have to be?"

Back home, Britain's Foreign Office and the London press were observing the news reports with mixed feelings. Diana's enormous worldwide popularity was obviously an asset in maintaining a good image for England and the Royal Family, but British diplomats in Washington were increasingly concerned that all this favorable publicity for Diana was not particularly beneficial for Prince Charles.

A week later, she was in Rome for another cancer fund-raiser, this time a banquet ($10,000 a plate) with extravagant courses left untouched by those glamorous guests obsessed with diets. "I have the greatest admiration for people like yourself who overcome all adversity," the Princess had written to Wendy Watson, the bold British campaigner for breast cancer research who had recommended her for the event. "You devote your life to such a wonderful and important cause."

Before the dinner in Rome, young, jaded Italian models—all of them from shabby-genteel Italian nobility—sauntered in summer outfits at the French Embassy. As usual, Diana was mobbed by journalists and paparazzi, perhaps even more so that evening since her dress revealed more of the royal bosom than had ever been seen in public.* Gazing at the bone-thin models, and apparently referring to her own past battles with anorexia and bulimia, Diana asked a reporter if he thought that the "poor waif look" should be banned from the fashion industry.

Since her marriage in 1981, Diana's involvements with charitable organizations had raised hundreds of millions of pounds annually for people ill, displaced by war or enduring alcohol, drug or mental prob-

---

*The word *paparazzi* comes into English via Italian. In 1959, Federico Fellini gave the name *Paparazzo* to a greedy photojournalist in his film *La Dolce Vita; paparazzi,* of course, is the plural form. Fellini had taken his cue from his cowriter, Ennio Flaiano, who had come across the name of a character, Coriolano Paparazzo, in a nineteenth-century novel by George Gissing titled *By the Ionian Sea.*

lems. For the British Red Cross alone, her presence brought £95 million in 1995; for Help the Aged, £50 million. The list of agencies whose reports she carefully read runs to three single-spaced pages.

Among those causes close to her heart were the emotional problems that led to anorexia and bulimia (of which she knew firsthand) and the plight of the homeless (of which she had learned a great deal).

"Many would like to believe," she said in remarks she prepared with help from a speechwriter but to which she always gave a personal turn, "that eating disorders are merely an expression of female vanity—not being able to get into a size-ten dress and the consequent frustrations. But eating disorders show how individuals can turn the nourishment of the body into a painful attack on themselves, and they have at their core a far deeper problem than mere vanity."

And the previous winter, when Diana visited a shelter for homeless drug addicts, she was visibly moved when she spoke. "It is truly tragic to see the total waste of so many young lives, of so much potential. Everyone needs to be valued. Everyone has the potential to give something back, if only they had the chance. Each time I visit here, I am appalled at the dangers young people face on the streets and how vulnerable they are to exploitation."

It was precisely to such causes that Diana had given her name in recent years—and not only her name, but her time and energy. She did not have to do this to be admired. She was already, for very many people round the world, not just a princess, but the "Queen of People's Hearts," which, as she had said in a television interview in 1995, was her fondest wish.

Hours after a last press reception for the fashion show in Rome, Diana arrived back in London. The following day, at her Kensington

Palace apartment near the western end of Hyde Park, she met with the heiress Aileen Getty. Once Elizabeth Taylor's daughter-in-law and still the actress's good friend, Getty had been suffering dreadful complications from AIDS for seven years.

By month's end, Getty was in the Mortimer Market Centre, an AIDS clinic ceremonially opened by Diana in 1994. Long before that time, she had famously shaken hands—without gloves—and leaned close to dying patients. So doing, she had made a dramatic point about the safety of human contact with those suffering social stigma as well as a morbid disease.

After Diana's visit with Getty, a reporter asked the Princess if she was "bowing to gay propaganda" by supporting the claim that AIDS widely affects not only homosexuals but segments of the entire world population. Diana flashed her sympathetic, intelligent blue eyes and replied firmly, "I am aware of that criticism, but I am determined to stick to my guns. Those who are ill are ill, and they all have a right to our compassion. That should be our only concern."

AIDS had been a special cause for Diana since the early days of its appearance, and she was always unafraid to give her embrace and her name to the battle against it. While on holiday on Martha's Vineyard in the summer of 1994, for example, Diana met Elizabeth Glaser, who had contracted the disease from a blood transfusion and unknowingly transmitted it to her two children. Glaser founded the Pediatric AIDS Foundation and became a crusader—as did Diana, who befriended Glaser and worked to raise money all over the world.

When the two women met that summer day, they spoke of their children—and especially of Ariel Glaser, who had died in 1988. "Diana and Elizabeth recognized how important it is to help children," said Paul Michael Glaser, the actor and Elizabeth's husband. "Diana acted from the heart; my wife did, too."

That autumn, Elizabeth Glaser's health took a sharp decline. When she could no longer speak, Paul or a friend held the telephone so she could hear Diana calling, encouraging her with sentiments of admiration and devotion. She died in December 1994, but not before turning the foundation into a major research organization. Diana remained a sympathetic friend to the Glaser family.

It was becoming clear—despite the insistent shattering of every illusion with which she had been raised and the heartache that had dogged her steps throughout her marriage—that Diana was finding her own clear path and her own clear accents. Often invited to speak in public, she wanted very much to refine that voice literally, and to this end she summoned an American communications consultant named Richard Greene, who had come to lunch in June to discuss public speaking. Arriving at Kensington Palace, he observed the formalities, addressing her (scant days before her loss of status) as Your Royal Highness. "Oh, please," she said, rolling her eyes and dazzling him with her smile, "call me Diana."

In fact, Diana's diction was clear and appealing as it was—refreshingly different from the upper-class tones that inflected the Prince of Wales (who sounded like a BBC radio commentator, circa 1934) and the Queen (who spoke like a suspicious and precise schoolteacher, circa 1910). Still, Diana was eager to improve. "I would love to be more comfortable speaking," she told Greene. "I envy Prince Charles's ability to stand right up there and tell jokes with such ease." Greene told her that the secret to effective public speaking, which should be easy for her to master, was simply caring about the topic at hand. "I do care," she replied. "They just don't seem to want to believe it." It was unclear whether "they" referred to the Royal Family, the world at large or, specifically, the badgering and often unkind press.

Sensibly, Diana and her tutor did not rush straight into lessons or exercises: they talked through the afternoon. She discussed her children, her charities—and love. "I think romance is overstated. I think now that what I really want is someone who can be a lifelong friend." Then as always, however, her favorite topic was her children.

In fact, Diana had begun diction and speaking lessons shortly after her marriage, and her mentor was none other than Sir (later Lord) Richard Attenborough. At first, he found her shy and nervous, and he considered that his task was to bolster her self-confidence. "My overwhelming impression was of an enchanting, somewhat wicked sense of humor, most often applied to herself." Contrary to the conventional wisdom about Diana—a tradition she herself encouraged by maintaining that she was "thicker than two planks"—Attenborough found her "truly intelligent, certainly not academic but somehow profoundly intuitive with an ability to master any brief on any subject with impressive skill."

On July 1, 1996, Diana marked her thirty-fifth birthday, but no special celebration was planned. In the morning, she visited the Chelsea Harbour Club for a workout, sprinting as usual from her car to the gym in a desperate attempt to avoid photographers. Later, she had lunch with her older son, Prince William, who had just turned fourteen; eleven-year-old Harry was still at school. He did not want to be king, William had told his parents earlier that year. He wanted a normal life, not one made ragged by flashbulbs and reporters. As he had remarked to Charles's courtiers during a recent luncheon in Norfolk when the conversation turned to the cost of fame, "Mummy had to pay a very high price."

This statement had touched Diana's heart, and although she told friends she would certainly consider leaving England permanently with her two boys—to avoid the ever more voracious press—she knew that such a step would guarantee neither safety nor privacy. Besides, it was out of the question: according to a venerable royal decree, she was even prevented from taking the boys on a foreign holiday without the Queen's explicit permission, which had just now been denied when she asked to take them to Atlanta for the summer Olympics.

Two days later, Diana was back in the thick of her charitable events, at least partly (thought her friends) to distract herself from the nastiness of the impending final divorce decree. An anti-gun lobby from Northern Ireland visited her at Kensington Palace, where she offered cold drinks and biscuits to the survivors of children killed in The Troubles.

"Where do you keep your crown?" asked a nine-year-old.

"I don't always wear it," replied Diana, smiling at the boy's parents. "Actually, I've left it in the car," she teased, gladly signing photographs for her visitors—just as, earlier that day, she had sent a note and a photo to a fifteen-year-old girl dying of leukemia.

On Friday, July 4—American Independence Day, as it was pointed out—documents from Prince Charles's lawyers were delivered to Diana's representatives; at that hour, she was dressing for a charity dinner. A week later, Their Royal Highnesses the Prince and Princess of Wales announced, through their press representatives, that they had agreed on the terms of a divorce settlement to be handed down in late August. The processing fees for the paperwork of the decree totaled £100, or about $160. No one breathed a deeper sigh of relief than Her Majesty the Queen, who had been pushing them both to get the divorce over and signed. In the estimation of one royal correspondent close to Buckingham Palace, "The Queen is frightened of Diana's influence on the public, which she does not want to be used against the Royal Family."

That same July night, the Princess attended a banquet across Hyde Park—at the Dorchester Hotel, where 600 guests including Mick Jagger and Jemima Khan joined her in raising funds for a Pakistani hospital.

A few months earlier, Diana had visited that same hospital, where there was a young boy with a festering tumor on his face. The sight and smell of the disease were appalling. "The boy could not open his mouth," recalled Dr. G. M. Shah, the hospital's medical director. "One eye was closed. It was not a happy scene. But she picked up that child and held him on her lap throughout a party we had for the children in the ward. She was happy to keep that poor child, whom so many people avoided, with her during the entire function. And she remembered his case when she returned to us later. He had died after her first visit, and when I told her this, she couldn't speak."

Separated almost four years (and in fact living apart very often since 1987), Charles and Diana were at last ready to conclude one of the most bitter and public matrimonial battles in history—a dispute both parties had waged more on television than in their attorneys' offices. There had been open admissions of infidelities by both husband and wife; each of them had authorized books detailing the shameful treatment which the other had meted out; and friends as well as professional royal watchers had divided into separate camps.

The material of the settlement seemed astonishingly prodigal in some ways and intolerably vindictive in others.

Diana would receive the equivalent of $28 million cash—nothing close to what her advisors had hoped, but enough to maintain a royal lifestyle. This would be invested, to guarantee an annual income of at least half a million pounds for the rest of her life and to cover $50,000 a year for clothes, $15,000 for hair and beauty maintenance and $40,000 a year for holidays. Her former husband agreed to pay for the education of their children, as well as for Diana's offices and staff.

She was granted permission to retain the spacious double apartment that she, her husband and the children had occupied in London at Kensington Palace; Charles would relocate to St. James's Palace, closer to "Buck House," as the family calls Buckingham Palace. At "KP," she would have the use of four reception or living rooms, a dining room, a master bedroom suite, two guest bedrooms, rooms for her sons (she would share equal custody rights) and staff accommodations. These were hers without fee.

But she would have to relinquish her status: Her Royal Highness Princess Diana of Wales would henceforth be known simply as Diana, Princess of Wales. Even that might have been wrested from her had she not been the mother of the two young princes, William and Harry, second and third in the line of succession to the throne of England after their father. As it was, this remarkably spiteful gesture may have been the Royal Family's single greatest tactical error since they allowed Prince Andrew to marry Sarah Ferguson, a woman with a checkered past and an impetuous, self-absorbed present. That *her* royal title would be withdrawn struck most people as simple justice. Diana was another matter entirely: she seemed more royal than the royals.

But to the Queen, immured in a lifetime of protocol and dusty royal attitudes, the sooner Diana was forgotten, the better. The Queen Mother, too—still one of the most powerful influences within the family—held Diana responsible for the public relations troubles the House of Windsor had been experiencing. This, of course, was rubbish: the Royal Family was doing a fine job of self-destruction even before Diana's arrival, merely by their raffish, garish irrelevance. They did not need the sympathetic Diana, clearly a modern woman longing to shine light on an archaic institution, to help diminish their currency.

Furthermore, as if to rub salt in the wounds, the Palace also announced that Diana's name would no longer be included in the Court Circular—the list of the Royal Family's official engagements, published six days a week. She may have done more good work in more venues than all members of the family combined, but the Palace press office seemed to be trying to insure that the world would know none of it from them. It hardly mattered. Like it or not, Diana had the media of the world at her door every time she so much as stepped out for tea.

In a meaningless nod, Buckingham Palace announced that Diana would retain her titles (if not her rank): she would still be the Countess of Chester, Duchess of Cornwall, Duchess of Rothesay, Countess of Carrick and Baroness Renfrew. It is doubtful that many outside the offices of *Burke's Peerage* had the remotest idea of the meaning of these labels. "I don't need another title," Diana told journalist Richard Kay. "I was born with one." She may also have known that her son, once he ascends the throne, might well restore the privilege: there was no historical precedent for a monarch's mother to be denied a royal title.

In addition, the gems Diana had received as gifts from the Queen, the Queen Mother and other members of the Royal Family from the time of her engagement through the years of her marriage to Charles— priceless jewels set in necklaces, tiaras, bracelets and brooches—would be hers to use during her lifetime. But the collection (assessed at something like $8 million) would revert to the Windsors at the time of her death, presumably to be passed on to her sons' wives.

On Wednesday, August 28, at precisely 10:27 in the morning, the final divorce decree was granted, and Diana Frances Spencer Windsor became perhaps the most eligible single mother in the world. She also joined the ranks of other divorced members of the royal family: Princess Margaret (the Queen's sister), Princess Anne (the Queen's daughter), Prince Andrew (the Queen's second son). But none of these caused the international reverberations of Diana's situation, for she was now the *former* wife of the future king of England.

Diana did not have to worry about earning a living for herself and her sons, but she was very much concerned about how to make a life. This was neither the first nor the last time she would have to face such a challenge.

4

IN THE SPIRIT OF ALIX

It would take the pity of God to get to the bottom of things.

—ENID BAGNOLD, *The Chalk Garden*

September 1996

With their divorce final by the end of August 1996, Charles and Diana were free to pursue their own lives and intimacies more openly, whereas before they had to exercise caution.

Even if he had been inclined to indifference about his own publicity, the newspaper reports of September 1 would have startled the Prince. A national survey reported that 54 percent of Britons said Charles must abdicate his claim to the throne if he were to marry Camilla Parker Bowles; 77 percent believed Charles lacked sufficient public respect to be an efficient king; and 79 percent said flatly they would not accept Camilla as his queen. Contrariwise, people were overwhelmingly sympathetic to Diana, who had been mistreated by the Windsor clan from day one and was now legally separated from them. But to his great surprise, Charles was enthusiastically mobbed by cheering crowds in Germany. After speaking at a summer engineering institute about the links between ecology and architecture, Charles stood on a balcony and waved to the smiling students below. "He's in very good spirits," one of his staff told the German press. "He goes down very well in Germany, but we certainly didn't expect *this*."

As summer turned to autumn, Diana kept a low profile. She canceled a portion of a hectic speaking schedule drawn up for the season, preferring instead to have quiet evenings with a few friends and to bring her boys from school to Kensington Palace for weekends of movies and picnics. But she was not isolated from the pain of others. At precisely this time, Diana began the habit of frequently slipping out of Kensington Palace late at night and arriving unannounced a few minutes later at the Brompton Hospital. There, in the deepest quiet of the night, she astonished the nurses by asking them to bring her to the loneliest and sickest patients, who must often have thought they were hallucinating when they opened their eyes to see the Princess of Wales sitting quietly at the bedside. Adele McCaffrey, who was among the staff there, recalled the many visits Diana made without fanfare.

This sort of thing simply was not done by members of the Royal Family, who always appeared according to a carefully orchestrated and scripted panoply. Diana was turning up not only at ballets and school openings but also, unheralded, in AIDS wards and cancer clinics, where she hugged babies and embraced adults.

And to her rounds she brought a refreshing sense of humor. Jonathan Grimshaw, at the Terrence Higgins Trust, recalled Diana's lack of royal protocol. Approaching the door of an AIDS hospice via the pebbled driveway, she had caught an annoying stone in her shoe. "The first thing she did inside," said Grimshaw, "was to pull the stone out of her shoe, hand it over with a smile and say, 'I think this belongs to you.' We had been terribly nervous, but she broke the ice immediately."

Her friends now were not the old landed gentry or the titled, mustached bores she knew as a child. She was drawing near to all those in need. "Nothing gives me greater joy than to try to help the most vulnerable members of society," she said a few days before her death. "It's my one real goal in life—like a destiny. Whoever is in distress and calls me—I'll run at once, wherever they may be."

It would be easy, in these mean-spirited times, to cast a critical, suspicious eye on activities and words like these, especially from a beautiful and desirable woman who lived in a cocooned world of luxury and abundance, who constructed a social world entirely according to her own tastes and who never knew any material deprivation. However, cynicism is out of order precisely because, since 1993, most of her attention went into direct contact with the people benefiting from her favorite charities—not merely board meetings, dinners and fashion shows—and because she troubled herself to visit the most unfortunate and shunned members of the modern world, wherever they might be.

Diana went, especially in the latter part of her life, where very few people wanted to go. It may be fashionable to loan one's name to a respectable charity dinner, but it is quite another matter to embrace African babies covered with AIDS wounds and Indian patients with leprous sores; to cradle children with terminal cancer and then to maintain contact with their grieving parents; to send handwritten notes to families shattered by sorrow at home and afar; to condemn openly the senseless border wars defended by politicians as "matters too complicated for the Princess to understand." Such an enormous and impressive network of concerns places her on the level of a real missionary, not the doyenne of paper foundations.

As for her fame, she was ruthlessly on target: "Always being in the public eye gives me a special responsibility—specifically, to use photo opportunities to send a message, to sensitize the world to an important cause or to defend certain values. People ask if I am an ambassador or a minister without portfolio. I prefer to define my role as that of a messenger."

If Diana was serving only the cause of her own publicity, she chose a remarkably ineffective means to achieve that. She knew only too well that real sacrifice, translating good intentions into hard work, is often maligned for the simple reason that people are made uncomfortable by being challenged. Not everyone has the time, the forum, the strength or the gift to devote to such extravagant good works, but everyone has the opportunity and the mandate to do *something:* that was what she wanted to communicate. Fund-raising dinners and charity fashion shows were fine as far as they went, but they did not go nearly far enough for her.

There were perhaps two main, ardent desires motivating Diana: she wanted a glamorous and exciting life, but she also wished to transcend it by a deeper commitment to causes and things that really matter. Here she is, photographed with Gianni Versace at his autumn fashion show; and there she is, filmed with Mother Teresa in one of the poorest sections of New York. Diana is the link between those two worlds—between merely temporal values and the eternal concerns. She had one beautifully attired foot in the world of glamour (the glitter that mirrors self-love) and the other sensibly shod foot firmly planted in the world of unconditional compassion (which reflects divine love). When she died, she was working out the perennial battle for ascendancy that wages in every soul.

Real goodness of spirit, for perhaps every human being, lies not in achieving what the medieval mystics called heroic sanctity; it lies in acknowledging that there is always a conflict, that one is always doing spiritual battle. The recognition that this is so—that one is always at work, never fully achieved—takes courage, one of many admirable qualities Diana possessed in abundance.

This is why it is foolish to ask whether she performed good deeds out of undiluted altruism or for her own emotional benefit—as if anyone could ever act from entirely pure motives. "Only God is love right through," as Thomas More famously said. The rest of us do what we can with our mixed reasons, trying, when we can, to bend selfishness into benevolence.

By September 1996, Diana's charity work had become a genuinely spiritual endeavor, as if by attending the fear and pain others endured she could deal more bravely with her own. You could say she was doing the royals one better, for it was in her role as the Princess of Wales that the family first moved her into the stream of their official good works. Little did they imagine how she would take to the tasks, affecting for good the institution that had rejected her, which was, ironically, the institution to whose fealty her sons were destined.

"You might say of her," commented the respected *Daily Telegraph* columnist Lord Deedes during the last year of Diana's life, "that she lost a husband and a position and is looking for a serious role. She remains, in my mind, extremely important because she is a very big influence in the life of Prince William, about whom she thinks a great deal, of whom she's very proud, and of whom she wants to make something very worthwhile. She wants to set an example to her sons—her older son in particular—which may produce a more sympathetic person. I think compassion is what she's trying to bring to her son's life." Diana did not, she made clear before and behind the scenes, wish William and Harry raised in the same frigid and authoritarian tradition that had bled so much of the humanity from their father's family. Several hundred years ago, civil war might have attended her style, let alone her late substance.

One striking example of Diana's empathy was evident that September when she attended the funeral of a student she had met at the Brompton Hospital—a twenty-seven-year-old named Yannis Kaliviotis, who had suffered from cystic fibrosis and was brought home to Greece for burial. Diana traveled with her friend Suzy Kassem (also a hospital visitor) to the island of Evia, where she was deeply moved by the devotion of the boy's family, for they would not allow the international press access to the church, nor would they permit photographs of them with their famous visitor.

She was grateful for what she learned about true religious dedication, Diana told Hillary Rodham Clinton at a White House breakfast that same month, within days of the Greek sojourn. Diana had agreed to attend a fund-raiser for breast cancer research, and she would not let exhaustion and a patch of the blues prevent her. "From where I sit," Diana said in her remarks at the dinner that evening, "I sense that the real fight against breast cancer has just begun. That is why I was so happy to accept this invitation from Kay [Graham] to share this evening with you." She then read a short verse that had special meaning for her—and, she said she believed, it might have equal meaning for everyone who comes to a fork in the road of life:

Life is mostly froth and bubble,
Two things stand in stone:
Kindness in another's trouble,
Courage in your own.

To find something like her equivalent in the English Royal Family, we have to go back to another Princess of Wales—Alexandra, who later became Queen when her husband was King Edward VII, from 1901 to 1910. "Alix," as she was affectionately called (the "Di" of her day), was a Danish princess who was brought to England to marry Queen Victoria's son. Beautiful and stately despite deafness and lameness, she was entirely devoted to her children and attended the wounded of the world right up to her death in 1925—an event that brought historic numbers of mourners to the streets of London when she was buried on a bitterly cold autumn day. It was Alexandra who brought the Royal Family into the twentieth century.

Diana revived the effort. But because she took advantage of all the modern means and exploited her beauty and fame to do so, the Royal Family deeply resented her, for Diana revealed to the Windsors and their courtiers their hopeless incompetence in dealing with the world and their spiritual inadequacy in communicating either example or a living tradition. To put the matter briefly, she bridged the wide gaps of a system more estranged from ordinary people than any institution since the court of Louis XVI.

But for all her good works, stern criticism was close at hand—as it happened, from no less a person than the Archbishop of Canterbury, who had married her to the prince fifteen years earlier. Lord Runcie's authorized biography, published that same September, indicated that the primate of England knew the marriage had been arranged, but that he believed she would fare well with some encouragement. By the early 1990s, according to the Archbishop, Charles had all but given up his faith in the Church of England and its doctrines—a singularly inauspicious development, Runcie believed, in light of the fact that Diana was so ignorant of religion and yet was trying to learn a thing or two. She was, felt the Archbishop, an actress and a schemer. This assessment, as he might have predicted, did nothing to warm Diana's relations with Christian clergymen.

On her return to London from Washington before the month's end, Diana may have been amused when the newspapers reported a kind of Royal Family summit at Balmoral in September. A committee (*committee!*)—consisting of the Queen, Prince Philip, their four children and various court officials—gathered to examine the future of the monarchy. This they did by planning public engagements for the next two years; arguing about a streamlining of the Changing of the Guard ceremony; and considering the pace at which Charles might introduce Camilla into royal social circles. If this accounting accurately reflects the Windsors' agenda, it serves to illuminate how out of touch the family is with the concerns and needs of their subjects *and* with the country's ongoing love affair with the beautiful and popular Diana.

As usual, the Windsors believed they could summon the press to support them when they wished and would be left alone when they preferred privacy. "I wish you would go away," snapped Queen Elizabeth II, whirling around to confront a gaggle of reporters who had followed her during a holiday at Sandringham in January 1981. Within five years, this was Her Majesty's reaction to her daughter-in-law Diana. For one thing, Diana had the unusual ability of blocking out attention that might have been given to anyone else in her presence. This she did not do by design, but by the sheer force of her ingenuous personality.

So much became clear even before the great royal wedding of 1981, when Charles and Diana attended a benefit concert at London's Goldsmith Hall. In a provocatively elegant off-the-shoulder black chiffon gown, Diana was cheered wildly; Charles, meanwhile, was only politely applauded. Amused (until such appearances by his wife stole virtually all of his thunder), Charles turned back to the photographers as the couple was whisked into the concert and asked, rather condescendingly: "Have all the fashion writers finished?" By the time of the wedding on July 29, Charles had become accustomed to the pattern of what would become the future. "I'll just have to get used to the backs of photographers when she is near me," he said to an aide.

For a comparison, one recalls the ill-fated January 1954 wedding of Marilyn Monroe, then twenty-seven, to Joe DiMaggio, who was almost forty. Like Charles, the baseball player's life had reached its fullness, had achieved something of a plateau; their beautiful brides, however, were just gaining their ascendancy. Of the two grooms the world knew very much indeed in 1954 and 1981; of their ladies the public knew little and longed for more.

The marriage of Charles and Diana, held at St. Paul's Cathedral because it accommodated more guests and was a better television location than Westminster Abbey, was broadcast to 750 million people worldwide. "A princely marriage is the brilliant edition of a universal fact," wrote the constitutional historian and scholar Walter Bagehot in 1867, "and as such it rivets mankind."

Indeed. The sheer brilliance of the lighting at St. Paul's, the cheers of the multitudes outside, the array of the entire Royal Family inside, the great throng of carriages, the processions of uniforms, the stately music, the attendance of heads of state, the bride with her twenty-five-foot-long train—the details fulfilled everything the pro-monarchists might have longed for. Nothing as grand and moving as this had occurred since the Queen's coronation twenty-eight years earlier, and the wedding of the Waleses had everything—it even seemed, to an unwitting world, to have love. However, Diana's devotion was not reciprocated, as the groom himself would admit to the world years later.

But no one could have known this at the time. Much of the appeal of the new Princess of Wales relied on the fact that, at twenty, she was young and beautiful and innocent. And so on her could be pinned all the hopes and dreams of every observer, and the fantasies of every woman. Even the Archbishop of Canterbury's wedding homily spoke of the event as the stuff of fairy tales.

"Well, she's going to have to learn to get used to this sort of thing," said the Queen with a sigh as she watched her daughter-in-law on television, coping with crowds in Wales and abroad that summer and autumn of her marriage. Diana, pink and pregnant by the end of 1981, was everywhere surrounded by a crush of photographers as if she were a carcass at the mercy of marauding ravens. And so it went, through the birth of Prince William in June 1982 and of Prince Henry (always called Harry) in September 1984. "Royal firstborns may get all the glory, but second-borns enjoy more freedom," said Diana. "Only when Harry is a lot older will he realize how lucky he is not to have been the eldest. My second child will never have quite the same sort of pressure that poor William must face all his life."

There was a strong undercurrent of autobiography here, for although three years of marriage had accustomed Diana to constant publicity, she had, by 1984, to face considerable unhappiness—not to say monumental boredom. In addition, every expectation of love and emotional support had been denied her.

For one thing, her husband's ongoing affair with Camilla Parker Bowles: of her marriage, Diana said on British national television that "with three of us in it, the marriage was a bit crowded." The comfort she had failed to find in that marriage she sought, over the years, from her children and friends and from the satisfaction of doing good works. She was also vulnerable to the blandishments of the glamorous

life: clothes, parties, expensive travel, gifts—like Candide's Cune-
gonde, she was not averse to glittering and feeling gay.

＊

Almost immediately after her honeymoon, Diana had learned that
her husband had no intention of giving up his mistress simply because
he was married. This might have devastated any but the most calculat-
ingly independent, unloving or masochistic wife. But to Diana, hypersensitive to the reactions of others and fiercely reliant on the approval
of those she loved and respected, this discovery was devastating. She
had believed in the fairy tale, and now it had proved an illusion. "I was
innocent," she said later, wistfully. "I felt that I was on cloud nine during our courtship simply because I was in the arms of the man I adored
and who, I believed, loved me. I believed that feeling would continue
forever."

It was perhaps no surprise to her family and friends, then, that by
the mid-1980s Diana was caught in a spiral of bulimia, clinical depres-
sion, panic-inducing anxiety and, still later, ill-advised love affairs.
Feeling unattractive and unwanted, she became obsessed with thin-
ness, which had become for many women a passport (so they thought)
to finding and receiving true love. At the same time—what else could
she do?—Diana's loneliness pitched her into a series of doomed
adventures (some of them perhaps platonic, some of them certainly
carnal) with entirely unsuitable men who could not offer the stability
she needed. There were entanglements with (among perhaps a few
others) the heir to a gin fortune (James Gilbey, the partner in the infamous "Squidgy" taped conversations); a royal riding instructor (James
Hewitt); a fashionable art dealer (Oliver Hoare); a rugby champion
with whom she may not, in fact, have spent much time at all (Will

Carling); and a millionaire playboy with whom she apparently did (Dodi al-Fayed).

A child of her generation, Diana had been raised with none of the usual securities of family, church or society. Now she raced from the gymnasium (to tone her body) to a therapist (to cleanse her soul); from her astrologer (to divine the future) to her aromatherapist (to apply calming, scented oils to her skin); from her nutritionist (for advice about the transforming effects of fiber in the diet) to the courtiers (to learn what was expected of her by a coldly indifferent Buckingham Palace staff). Constantly on the go, ravenous for peace and unmindful of where it might be found, Diana had turned thirty in 1991 with no clear idea of what, if any, function she might have in the world.

Charles might have wondered the same of himself. His mother, suffering from an excess of zeal and a distrust that anyone but herself was fit to be monarch, denied him any effective role and consigned him to polite uselessness. Prevented from political involvement as well as from holding down a responsible job, Charles could only cultivate harmless hobbies, utter banalities on command and conduct an affair with his heart's true love.

But this did not, apparently, make him happy, and so Charles became a somewhat dreary figure, tugging obsessively at his cuffs and necktie and casting a disconsolate eye on a world he longed to understand but could not. "Women adore him," said Lord Charteris, a close friend of the Queen and one of her secretaries for over a quarter century. "Charles is such a charming man—when he isn't being whiny."

By 1994, the Prince and Princess of Wales had been separated for almost two years, and they maintained independent courts and homes—his at St. James's Palace and Highgrove, hers at Kensington Palace. From this time, Charles's whining became remarkably public. On June 29, for example, he told the world—on television, as his family watched, horrified—that he had been unfaithful to his wife because his marriage had "irretrievably broken down"—a confession made, it seems, without regard for its subsequent effect on his children.

Wanting everyone to understand the depth of his unhappy past and the distress of his uncertain present, he said that he felt he had to justify his existence; one might have replied that he ought to consider another job. Until this point, he had shared his deepest feelings only with Camilla, but now (what the hell) he told the world. Diana was not the only one aware of the power of the media, nor the only one to exploit it for her own purposes. But in her favor it must be said that she did not make herself look foolish, perhaps because she did *not* try to justify.

At the same time, Charles was meeting with his authorized biographer, who was putting finishing touches to a book intended to improve the Prince's popularity rating. He had felt unloved in childhood, the Prince said through journalist Jonathan Dimbleby; he had never really loved his wife, whom he married from a sense of duty. "How *could* I have got it all so wrong?" he asked plaintively. Easy if you know how, his royal ancestors might have replied across the frontiers of time and history.

It was not long, of course, before the divorce of Mr. and Mrs. Parker Bowles was announced, too. "Of course she is the love of Charles's life," continued Lord Charteris as the world eagerly awaited each installment of the saga.

No one had to wait very long. James Hewitt, once an equestrian in the Queen's Household Division and a riding instructor to various royals, also took the swiftest contemporary route if you want easy money and have some sexy stories to peddle. Hewitt cooperated on a slim, breathless little volume detailing his occasional clandestine trysts with Diana between 1986 and 1991. Sounding like refugees from a quaintly inferior novella by D. H. Lawrence, Diana and Hewitt nicely counterbalanced Charles and Camilla. "This cannot go on," said the Queen, snapping off the television reports about Hewitt's book and ringing for her private secretary.

Little did she know. Speaking to the nation and the world in November 1995, Diana threw herself on the capacious mercy of the television camera and on the emotional largesse of a world that sympathizes with a beautiful victim. "Yes, I adored him," she said quietly. "Yes, I was in love with him. He was a great friend of mine at a very difficult time," said Diana on the program *Panorama,* admitting her affair with James Hewitt, "and he was always there to support me. But I was very let down. I was absolutely devastated when this book appeared, because I trusted him and because I worried about the effect on my children. He rang me up ten days before it arrived in the bookshops to tell me there was nothing to worry about, and I believed him, stupidly. When the book did arrive, the first thing I did was rush down to talk to my children. And William produced a box of chocolates and said, 'Mummy, I think you've been hurt. These are to make you smile again.'"

The program and its unprecedented boldness shook Buckingham Palace but not the general population. Where Charles's admissions of infidelity were met with ridicule and contempt, Diana's gained even more sympathy for her than she had achieved previously. The applause could almost be heard when she protested, on the same television show, that she would "fight to the end, because I have a role to fulfill. I don't think I've been given any credit for growth. And my goodness, I've had to grow."

Yet this appearance was not an unqualified success, though, in an odd and perverse way, she had been trained to connect with the television audience by none other than Richard Attenborough.

"As a wounded animal, she could be terrifying," said her closest friend, Rosa Monckton, "and her infamous *Panorama* interview was an example of that. It was born of some basic desire to hurt those she felt had betrayed her. But she also had the ability to admit her mistakes, and she said to me that she regretted doing the program. The sad thing is that it was her only television interview, and it was Diana at her worst."

"A family on the throne is an interesting idea," mused Walter Bagehot in the last century. "And a Royal Family sweetens politics by the seasonable addition of nice and pretty events." Such a family, he continued, attracts the attention of the world because it reflects "the level of petty life." Writing in the time of Queen Victoria, he could not have foreseen just how petty the royal lives could become (rather than merely edifyingly ordinary), and how less nice and pretty the events.

By early 1995, Diana, wearing a shimmering, bare-backed and sequined gown with a thigh-high slit, had Paris in mute adoration: she, by now the world's favorite cover girl, was certainly not rejected by the French for her amours. "She draws interest wherever she goes and whatever she does," said her smiling hostess, former French first lady Anne Giscard d'Estaing. The charity event to which Diana came was held, aptly, in the Hall of Battles. She may have put some of the Gallic press and public in mind of the courts of Henry II and his estranged wife, Eleanor of Aquitaine: there were the same plots and schemes among their courtiers, the identical stratagems and wiles, whispering campaigns and vendettas.

Back in London, meantime, Charles kept his own strategy. To a man who said he had recently met Diana, he replied publicly, "You lived to tell the tale, did you?" Diana never stooped to this kind of sarcasm, at least not in the public forum. Simultaneously, their sons' schoolmates were taunting William and Harry about their parents' lovers.

To make matters worse for the palace, forty percent of the British public said in a poll that the monarchy ought to be abolished. Such a cry for a Republic of Britain was the loudest heard since Victoria's long, insistent retreat from public life in the nineteenth century. "The nation has turned as never before against the Prince of Wales," ran a typical news story, "and blames him for a series of catastrophic blunders that could bring about the fall of the House of Windsor within the next century."

Meanwhile, the public continued to sympathize with Diana, and perhaps with good reason. She admitted her failings, she was a devoted mother, she was victimized by power and glamour, she empathized with the poor and the outcast. And she was invariably lovely. There was something wholesome about her, something always dignified, something still undefiled despite her loss of innocence. There was nothing sleazy about her, and she never sank to nasty diatribe. Nor did she convey the shallow, goofy tartiness of her former sister-in-law Sarah Ferguson, the Duchess of York.

Diana's failings humanized her, and that, it always seemed, was how she best connected to people—not by standing on the ceremony of her royal prerogatives, and not by lowering herself to the lowest common denominator of bad deportment. Rather, she raised up everyone to her own level of warm dignity; she showed how people might stumble but survive. She made humanity shine out like a restored picture. No one minded (in fact most people seemed to appreciate) that she had the unlimited wealth to indulge all the means possible to survive and to grow.

Use the wealth and prestige she might—for herself and for others—but Diana never believed that any of it made her better than others, and this needs to be emphasized in any account of her life. Not long after her marriage, she had gone down to the kitchen at Balmoral Castle to greet the staff and to discuss her and Charles's favorite dishes. There was a shocked silence: all in attendance, save the Princess, knew that one of her staff ought to do this. As the visit was concluding, one of the senior attendants took her aside and said, "I must ask you not to come down here again, Ma'am. You are a royal, and you must never mix with us. We know our place—and we expect you to know yours." She returned to her rooms feeling more lonely and isolated than ever.

"That was so painful," she recalled later, and the incident was exacerbated when she saw that she was being virtually frozen out of the Windsors' life. "No one talks to me," she complained to one of Charles's cronies. "I stand around at every official gathering not knowing what to do, what to say or where to look. I'm worried that I might do something wrong, and I feel like the fish out of water."

When she stood around, however, she was at her easiest to document—and so she learned to stand around and smile, which she did superbly well. Always polite, she learned how to ingratiate, too: in a way, she learned to evoke from the press what she was not getting from her own family circle.

Hence the slightest sign of Diana's feelings was duly noted by the ever-present eye of the camera. A laugh, a frown, an indication of anger, pleasure or boredom—every word, glance and manner was parsed and interpreted for significance, every touch of her hand was considered a benediction. Nothing she did was unimportant. Very soon this produced the inevitable result: she both appreciated and resented the power of the press.

As this exposure intensified, Diana came to expect and need all this public attention—but she hated the concomitant scrutiny. She needed the waves of devotion that washed over her from society, who came to know her not in person but through those curious modern means, the television image and the luminous color photographs in slick magazines. These were a kind of substitute love for Diana, who had endured a broken home in childhood and then a rude shock when her marriage went sour. Afraid of repeating the mistake of her parents, she endured—at first in silence. Then her rebellion took an unexpected curve.

And so she became the goddess Diana, the enchantress who pursued love and approval by extending it to others: this was indeed a royal hunt, almost a kind of mystical pursuit. She was also, of course, radiant, exquisite, elegant, witty and warm, and—ever a child of her time—she easily revealed her emotions, as the royals simply do not.

But sometimes, during the years before her divorce was final, things were out of control. From 1981 to 1994 alone, she spent more than $2 million on her wardrobe, which also goes far toward explaining the attention lavished on her by photographers and fashion designers. At the beginning of 1995, Diana could count more than 3,000 outfits in her spacious closets, a fifty-yard length of ball gowns, 600 pairs of shoes and 400 hats. Her husband was speechless in the face of such prodigality: he owned three or four dozen suits and several standard uniforms and took little interest in what his valet laid out for him each day.

Diana's in-laws looked no more favorably on her chic than on her charm, and Windsor family gatherings, by 1996, left her chilled to the bone; she attended only when it was necessary for her children to be with her and the Queen simultaneously, which was not often. Diana found Sandringham like a third-rate hotel—damp, badly heated, inhospitable. As for Balmoral, that was merely the setting for tedious family gatherings. "Boring, raining," was her summary of one holiday there.

At first, Diana had been amused but later was irritated by the Queen's frugalities. She could not fathom why the monarch padded through unoccupied rooms switching off lights, nor could she ever accept the royal custom of reversing the bed linens to save on laundry bills. Once, Diana gently commented on the chilliness of a sitting room at Balmoral. "Put on another sweater," said the Queen with a prim smile. The diaries of visitors to the royal precincts doubtless groan with accounts of such eccentricities.

5

WORKING BY INSTINCT

Titles are shadows, crowns are empty things,
The good of subjects is the end of kings.

—DANIEL DEFOE, *The True-Born Englishman*

October—November 1996

He would like to be reincarnated as Diana, Princess of Wales, said Gianni Versace on October 1 at the presentation of his new collection in Milan. It would be the only way he would ever get to wear great clothes and to see them looking their finest. Responding to this broadcast news item, she sent him flowers and a wish to be reunited soon with Versace—perhaps at the Christmas holiday?

The next day, things turned bizarre.

Madame Vasso Kortesis, a peculiar Greek lady living in London, had been counseling Fergie as astrologer, psychic, card reader and general spiritual mother-figure. Now the guru had decided to go public with her story—hence another book about Prince Andrew's ex-wife.

The Duchess, who had foolishly agreed to allow her confidante to tape their conversations occasionally over the last seven years, was now reduced to sputtering rage as the British public could spend a few pounds and ring a pay-telephone line to hear excerpts. After a few days of damage, the law intervened, but a book was being hurriedly prepared.

The recorded chats were not mere enigmatic musings, they were lurid accounts of sexual escapades, and they brought support from Prince Andrew and from Diana—from him because the revelations were embarrassing to everyone in the family; from her because Diana was no stranger to the dusky drawing rooms of London's bizarre occultists, and she wondered if *she* had been taped, perhaps unwittingly.

Fergie was a hot little number, as the tapes revealed: she had chatted gaily to the mystic Madame about her trysts with Steve Wyatt, the Texas millionaire; with Andrew; with the financial adviser John Bryan; with an unnamed Arab billionaire; with a London artist; with an Austrian tennis champ; with an Irish riding instructor—her capers made Diana seem like a Carmelite nun.

But as it happened, Diana's consoling visit to the divorced Fergie was one of their last meetings. Next day, the press carried lengthy transcripts of the Vasso conversations with the Duchess that revealed the redhead's jealousy toward the one she contemptuously called "Blondie." With a touch of absurdity, Fergie added (with utter seriousness, insisted Madame) that one day she and Diana would fight for the affections of John F. Kennedy, Jr. Mr. Kennedy's reaction to this bizarre prediction has not been documented. Diana was able to avoid the London press in this matter by dashing off to Italy, where at Rimini she received an award for humanitarian service to the world.

To the astonishment of some, Buckingham Palace released a minor press item to the effect that the Queen was entirely sympathetic to the poor Duchess of York (not, however, to the extent of bailing her out of a two-million-dollar debt). "Of course, the Queen's feelings toward Fergie need to be seen in context," said someone disguised as an "informed source." And Her Majesty's real contempt was reserved for Diana, whom the Queen believed to be "scheming and devious, so anybody is bound to fare better than she in the monarch's estimation." The source added that both Diana and Fergie delighted in hearing reports about each other's discomfort, "because it takes the pressure off [each one's own trouble], at least temporarily."

Accepting the Italian award, Diana used the opportunity to speak about one of her favorite matters: the challenge of an aging population in developed countries. "There is always a temptation for each new generation to believe that it has all the answers, and that those who are older are obsolete," she said, reading from notes she had written that afternoon. "To regard old age as a disease, as many do, is to waste one of our greatest resources. To look down on the elderly as somehow out of touch is to disregard the fount of both wisdom and experience." She spoke fondly of her late father, who had died in 1992, and whom she missed every day of her life.

Well, said the heart transplant pioneer Dr. Christiaan Barnard, who was present at Rimini: now he understood why Diana was staking her claim to become the "Queen of People's Hearts," as she had said on television in November 1995. Some churlish journalists would not leave that self-designated title alone, and it became something of a nasty running joke.

The snide comments about Diana as the self-styled queen of people's hearts became more indelicate still on October 15, when the Queen had the last of several meetings with Betty Boothroyd, Parliament's senior constitutional expert. Miss Boothroyd, a stickler for propriety, agreed with Her Majesty that it was no longer appropriate to include the Princess of Wales in official prayers recited at the start of each business day in the Houses of Commons and Lords. Until then, the bidding prayers asked for blessings and guidance on the Queen, then on the Duke of Edinburgh, then on the Prince and Princess of Wales, then on "all members of the Royal Family." Members of Parliament returned from a summer recess, however, to find Diana stricken from the list of the day's formula orisons.

The entire petty business had something comically vindictive about it, not to say something profoundly unchristian. "They are trying to airbrush the Princess from the Establishment in a Stalinist manner," said Tory representative Jerry Hayes. Clearly, neither the Palace nor its spokesmen took very seriously the fundamental message of Jesus: to do good to those whom they considered enemies, to pray for those who caused hurt and to shower with goodwill those who are an embarrassment—they certainly considered Diana in that corner.

It is difficult to understand how omitting someone who is the mother of the future king of England from their prayers is designed to "respect protocol." It may have struck devout souls that something was radically wrong with this kind of thinking, especially on command of the Queen, Defender of the Faith. Signed by Her Majesty, the warrant striking Diana from the prayers was drawn up on the advice of the Archbishop of Canterbury with the agreement of senior Parliamentary ministers under the redoubtable Miss Boothroyd. Not everyone was polite about this: "It seems rather cold and cruel in view of the huge sadnesses the Princess has experienced," said Sir Teddy Taylor, Tory member of Parliament for Southend East.

But the Queen of Hearts faced forward with her usual quiet dignity, gauging the public's feelings far more accurately than did the Royal Family. At the end of October, via a television poll, Diana was named by 2,000 men and women as the perfect role model for

Diana on a visit to Northwick Park Hospital to lay a foundation stone for a new children's wing.

BELOW: Princess Diana attends the 30th anniversary of the International Leprosy Association in London on September 12, 1996.

ABOVE: Visiting the Viana Red Cross Handicap Hospital in Angola, January 12, 1997.

RIGHT: At a charity event for breast cancer, September 1996.

LEFT: At the Nina Hyde Breast Cancer Research fund-raiser with Anna Wintour and Ralph Lauren.

BELOW: Diana cradles a young child stricken with cancer during a show at a hospital in Lahore, Pakistan.

ABOVE: Arriving at a gala in Sydney, Australia, honoring the Victor Chang Cardiac Research Institute.

With Nevresa Bradaric, whose 14-year-old son is one of the many victims of land mines scattered all over Bosnia.

Diana attends the London premiere of *In Love and War,* February 12, 1997.

© AP / Wide World Photos.

© STEVE FINN / Alpha / Globe Photos, Inc.

In private moments, as well as public appearances, the paparazzi captured every move the Princess made. She is seen here outside her Chelsea gym; at the premiere of the English National Ballet of *Swan Lake*; and before leaving for a visit to Washington, D.C.

PERIGO MINAS!

DANGER   MINES

THE
HALO
TRUST

Diana in Angola to protest the use of land mines during a four-day visit to Southern Africa.

Spending time with a young patient at an orthopedic center outside the Angolan capital of Luanda, January 1997.

On a working visit to Luanda where 9 million land mines—one for every person in the country—still lie in wait for victims.

With Liz Tilberis at the Metropolitan Museum of Art's Costume Institute Gala honoring Christian Dior, September 9, 1996.

Escorting American land mine survivor Ken Rutherford, who has two artificial legs, to a meeting of the Red Cross in Washington, where the princess met with Red Cross President Elizabeth Dole to discuss land mines, January 17, 1997.

On her trip to Pakistan.

**Visiting the Shankat
Khanunu Memorial Cancer
Hospital and Research Center
in Lahore, Pakistan.**

**On July 1, 1997, the night of her
36th birthday, Diana attended
a charity event sponsored by
Chanel at the Tate Gallery
in London.**

Diana dashes through the crowds to the entrance of her gym in London, August 1997.

© Capital Pictures/Gamma Liaison, Inc.

© DAVE CHANCELLOR/Alpha/Globe Photos, Inc.

Being greeted by a young fan as she attends a private viewing of her collection of dresses to be auctioned off by Christie's.

Mother Teresa and Diana at the Missionaries of Charity in the South Bronx.

With Elton John at the memorial service
for their friend Gianni Versace, July 1997.

In Sydney, Australia,
November 1, 1996.

After addressing the
Red Cross gala event in
Washington, D.C., Diana
sits with Bob Dole.

In Chicago, June 1997, on a fund-raising visit for cancer research.

Speaking on behalf of land mine victims at a Red Cross fund-raiser in Washington, D.C., June 17, 1997.

Leaving the Mortimer Market Center, a London clinic for HIV/AIDS patients, June 27, 1996.

Diana and Dodi al-Fayed at the French Riviera resort of St. Tropez, August 22, 1997.

Princes William and Harry, with their father, Prince Charles, viewing the tributes left outside Kensington Palace in memory of their mother.

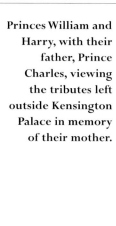

Prince William waiting to enter Westminster Abbey for the funeral service of his mother.

The Duke of Edinburgh, Prince William, Earl Spencer, Prince Harry and Prince Charles following the funeral cortege of Diana, Princess of Wales, September 6, 1997.

The coffin of Diana carried
by the bearer party of
Welsh Guardsmen into
Westminster Abbey
for her funeral.

As the funeral service
concludes, Diana's coffin is
carried out of the Abbey.

The Union Jack flies at half mast over Buckingham Palace as the hearse bearing Diana's body moves up the Mall, leaving London for her burial place at Althorp, the Spencer family estate.

The funeral cortege passes through the village of Harelstone, Northamptonshire, a mile away from the Althorp Estate, where Diana will be laid to rest.

women of the 1990s. With that endorsement and the humanitarian acclamation trumpeted side by side in the press, Diana departed for a four-day charity visit to Sydney, Australia. She could apparently do no wrong.

Her ex-husband, meantime, could do very little right. After undertaking ever more dangerous stunts on the polo field, Charles was openly accused of flirting with disaster—perhaps out of a frank death wish. He loved everything to do with gardens, but whereas his ancestors were admired for this typically English hobby, Charles was ridiculed. Did he not have better things to do than talk to his daisies?

At the same time, it was gleefully reported in the press that at Highgrove Charles had put into action the abstemious measures so beloved by his mother. Leftovers crammed the royal refrigerator, because he ordered that not a morsel of food be wasted; the result was that spoiled remnants caused more waste than if the first surplus had been given to servants or the poor. Then there was the price of fruit and poultry. From his car, Charles had spotted prices in a market; next day, chicken and apples were banned from Highgrove for a month.

These stories—some of them unfair exaggerations—contrasted heavily with the glorification of his former wife. Longing to break out of her gilded cage, Diana dismissed her bodyguards, which infuriated the Queen: she feared for the security of her royal grandsons when they were with their mother. But the public loved photos of Diana and her two boys at an amusement park, on a picnic or shopping. On such outings, she gave William and Harry cash and instructed them to line up at the register with other customers.

Wherever she went, people called out to her, and, often enough, she smiled, waved back and instructed the boys in proper manners toward the public. In this regard, it must be stressed that whatever Diana's personal resentments of the rotten treatment she received from the Windsors, she was punctilious in her duty to raise her sons as good royals whose future was intimately bound to the destiny of the throne. "Once or twice, I've heard people say that Diana's out to destroy the monarchy, which has me bewildered. Why would I want to destroy something that is my children's future?"

She did not, in other words, poison them against the very system that had meted out such harsh treatment to her. But sometimes she did ask photographers not to crowd her children too much. Sometimes, they complied, although in December 1993, one of the paparazzi promised, with a wink, that he and his telephoto lens would "follow Diana to the grave."

Dashing hither and thither, Diana seemed to look younger than ever, accepting the flowers thrust into her hands as if each bunch were the first bouquet she had ever seen. Poor Charles, meantime, seemed forever frozen in time, his hands invariably clasped behind his back or tucked into the pockets of his double-breasted suits. His wife's glamour and fame, as the Prince's authorized biographer attested, "sapped his confidence and made him long to escape" the prying eyes of the press. Of course, he could not, any more than could she. As he went about more openly with Camilla, he underestimated the resentment of the people. They were not ready to accept Mrs. Parker Bowles as a replacement for the beloved Diana.

These developments reached Diana on her Australian visit, whither she arrived on October 31 and whence she departed four days later. As it happened, the Australians were at the moment caught up in fierce public arguments about whether they ought to remain in the Commonwealth (which most politicians felt was to their economic advantage) or to sever ties with London once and for all. In light of this, Diana was, to her astonishment, not received as warmly as she might have been: people simply did not know what to make of her.

Things began routinely enough. At the Sydney Entertainment Centre, an evening ball was held to benefit the Victor Chang Cardiac Research Institute. A gifted heart surgeon who had been brutally murdered, Chang was the subject of Diana's brief remarks: "It has been said that for evil to triumph, good men must do nothing. Tonight we give heartfelt thanks that a good man, Dr. Victor Chang, did a great deal." Then, after dinner, a politician named Neville Wran (who longed to throw off the last vestiges of connection to England) squired Diana to the dance floor.

This was Wran's prerogative as chairman of the Research Institute. But the dance floor at once became crowded, and other guests swept down on Diana to cut in. Moments later, Diana returned to her table, collected her purse and her assistant and swept out of the room. Was she offended? No, replied an aide when the newspapers rang next day. She was exhausted from jet lag. But when Diana's schedule was rearranged next day, Aussie reporters felt she was offering a royal snub.

The truth was that they could not have been more wrong. Diana had been upset by a fax she had received before dinner from the press office at Buckingham Palace, implying that her visit to Australia had a detrimental effect on the Queen's state visit to Thailand, then also in progress. The reason for this embarrassment would not, of course, be entirely clear to anyone but Diana, the court and Parliament.

The state of the Commonwealth, essentially an economic partnership among countries once part of the Empire and now loosely bound by ties of more or less loyal confederation, is invariably a subject for the Queen to discuss, on counsel from the Prime Minister and the Foreign Secretary. It is not an area normally promoted by those outside the immediate royal circle (where Diana now stood). But Diana felt that her elder son's future role as head of this affiliation of fifty-three nations was significant and she had wanted to support its aims.

It was in this spirit—of her son's youth and of his future—that she spoke as a mother at the Commonwealth Day Council luncheon to raise funds for disadvantaged children. "As I am sure you know," she told the gathering in impromptu remarks and without reading from notes, "the Commonwealth has a very special place in the world of international relations. It gives a sense of belonging one to another, even though we live in different nations and continents. That sense of belonging is focused on the children of the Commonwealth."

However innocent, such remarks were regarded by politicians at home and even by some in Australia as astonishingly impertinent. But when Diana was hugged after her speech by a thirteen-year-old girl who had lost a leg to bone cancer, the tension was at once defused. And as a blind and paralyzed boy, injured in a sports accident, was wheeled up to her, Diana bent down, held the boy's withered hands, kissed him and spoke soothingly for a half hour to him and his parents. Was she now acting in defiance of protocol, too? Or was this not the authentically royal touch, and politics be damned? People were making their own decisions.

"Yes, I touch people, literally," Diana told an interviewer from *Le Monde* a few days before her death. "I think everyone needs that, whatever his age. To put your hand on the face of someone in trouble or sick or grieving—that is to have immediate contact, to communicate with tenderness, to indicate your nearness to people. It's a natural gesture that comes from the heart—it has no advance planning. And the truth is that I feel near to people who are suffering, whoever they are. That's why I disturb certain people, because I'm closer to the lowly than to the mighty, and they can't forgive me for that. I have an instant rapport with ordinary people. My father always taught me to treat everyone as an equal. I've always done that, and I'm sure that Harry and William have absorbed the same spirit. Well, no one can dictate my behavior to me. I work by instinct. It's my best advisor."

Then, as if on cue, the chains of Diana's problems with the tempestuous Duchess of York rattled from afar. While she was visiting an AIDS hospice in Sydney, Diana was informed that extracts from yet another book—one with the greasy title *Fergie: Her Secret Life*—were appearing on London newsstands. Dr. Allan Starkie, yet another "friend," adviser and confidant, claimed to be the spiritualist guru who had succeeded the disgraced Madame Vasso. He predicted that Prince Charles would die, that Andrew would be appointed to fill his place and that Fergie would thus at last outrank Diana.

The author described in breathless detail the Duchess's jealousy of Diana, as well as her anger, when the Princess leaked news of Fergie's separation to the press. There were also comments about her angry fits of crying when Diana received good media coverage or appeared on television. According to Starkie, Fergie believed she was really meant for Prince Charles—that her destiny was to be queen. If true, these aspirations give new meaning to Sarah Ferguson's galloping case of *folie de grandeur.* Quite apart from any judgment on the veracity or quality of the book, it had the effect of causing a permanent rupture in the fragile relations between the two ex-royals.

Nor was this healed by the publication of Fergie's own book, *My Story,* which was serialized in *Hello!* magazine that same month. Among other incidents, she reported how pleased she was when her former sister-in-law took the heat off the Duchess when Diana's loving, taped conversations with James Gilbey were the news of the day. In addition, Fergie described Diana as "teary, reclusive and out of sorts" whenever she was forced to attend a family visit to Balmoral. Poor, weak Diana, the book implied: she had not the stomach for royal encounters. Fergie had, after all, promised Diana she would not mention her in the book, and here she was . . .

By odd coincidence, the Diana-Gilbey affair had been publicized when an Australian magazine ran excerpts from the so-called Squidgy tapes, so named for his nickname for the Princess. The conversations had been recorded in 1989:

DIANA: I don't want to get pregnant.

GILBEY: Darling, that's not going to happen—all right?

DIANA: Yeah.

GILBEY: Don't look at it like that. It's not going to happen. You won't get pregnant.

DIANA: I watched *EastEnders* [a television series] today. One of the main characters had a baby. They thought it was by her husband. It was by another man.

GILBEY: Squidgy, kiss me. [Sounds of kissing over the phone lines.] Oh, God, it's wonderful, isn't it—this sort of feeling?

DIANA: I love it.

GILBEY: I know. Darling—it's more—it's just like sort of—

DIANA: Playing with yourself? [She giggles. And later, speaking of the Windsors:] This is all bloody hell—after all I've done for this fucking family! I can't stand the confines of this marriage. [Charles] makes my life real torture!

The Australians, never slow to poke the Royal Family, treated Diana with the utmost courtesy, but during her visit one or two magazines trotted out past evidence of troubles and infidelity.

As for the Duchess, she was asked flat out, while promoting her book in America, if she would like to move to the United States. "Like a shot," she told Diane Sawyer. "I love it over here. If it comes to a point where it works out that I can be abroad with my children, then abroad with my children it will be."

And then, all smiles, she moved in for the final volley. "Oh, Diana and I were the Thelma and Louise of Buckingham Palace," she said with a laugh. As the conversation then turned to questions about her wild overspending, she took aim at Diana's past problems: "A lot of people have done worse than overspend. You could be an addict of some sort, or you could be on drugs or I could, you know, have an equivalent of bulimia or something. I guess I've got overspending disease, you know? I just went mad—I spent too much." Perhaps someone ought to have told Fergie that she also occasionally spoke too much.

In fact, Diana made ever more impassioned speeches on behalf of women suffering the psychological and physical effects of eating disorders. One of the reasons for her great popularity in the last years of her life was that women in vast numbers could identify with the emotional turmoil of such illnesses. And women, especially, understood Diana's lack of self-confidence, a crisis based on an unhappy and emotionally deprived childhood, a disappointing marriage and a feeling of having to conform to unreal standards of beauty. Women also admired her attachment to her children and her craving to be loved, and they grasped what her brother called "her childlike desire to be rid of her deeply rooted feelings of unworthiness." Most of all, they respected her refusal to be overcome by her problems. Paradoxically, she also became more and more beautiful, more and more triumphant over the various systems that so often conspire to crush sensitive spirits.

Diana acknowledged that the press, in detailing her battles with bulimia, often stressed only the crude details and not the underlying traumas. "Ladies and gentleman," she had told those gathered at a women's charity called Well Being, "I think you are very fortunate to have your patron here today. I was supposed to have my head down the loo for most of the day. I'm supposed to be dragged off the minute I leave here by men in white coats. But if it's all right with you, I thought I might postpone my nervous breakdown."

That said in November 1993, Diana's courage had deepened by the month. She would not endure jokes or jabs about any illness—not only because she was hypersensitive for herself but also because she would not risk the hurt to any woman of similar experience. "I had bulimia for a number of years," added Diana in statements that drew the admiration and loyalty of millions of women around the world. "It's like a secret disease. You inflict it upon yourself because your self-esteem is at a low ebb and you don't think you're worthy or valuable. You fill your stomach up four or five times a day—some do it more— and it gives you a feeling of comfort. In my case, it was a symptom of what was going on in my marriage. I was crying out for help but giv-ing the wrong signals, and people were using my bulimia as a coat on a hanger—they decided that was the problem: Diana was unstable."

Along with the frankness that made her a role model of the vic-tim, of the survivor and of the triumph over all odds, Diana demon-strated a touching vulnerability. This was evident in her almost religious identification with emotionally damaged women: she knew that with just a little more stress or a little less support from her friends, she, too, might be a candidate for a nervous breakdown. "There seems to be a growing feeling of emptiness in people's lives," she had said recently at a mental hospital. "Deep within us all is a need to care and be cared for—yet many people, in their attempt to build a life, lose touch with their own sense of belonging and of being a part of something greater than themselves." She could have been speaking for herself, for being a part of something important that was greater than her own life occupied Diana's attention constantly during her last year.

The newspapers continued to annoy Diana when she returned from Australia to London on November 5, 1996. The Sunday *Mirror* reported that she was having an affair with the Pakistani cardiac surgeon, Dr. Hasnat Khan, who was thirty-six and whom Diana had met on hospital rounds in London. "I want to marry him and have his babies," said Diana, according to the paper. Did she indeed? asked a friend. "Bullshit," muttered Diana, and that was that. Tracked down at Harefield Hospital, the nervous Dr. Khan waved away reporters: "I am very busy. I cannot answer any questions."

As if the structural links were provided by a script, the Prince of Wales and Camilla decided to celebrate Charles's forty-eighth birthday at Highgrove with, of all things, an Indian-Pakistani theme. With Camilla as hostess and Ravi Shankar among the guests, forty invited friends drifted around the gardens and the dinner tables in traditional Indian garb. Dr. Khan was not among them.

Within the week, Diana was back on the luncheon and dinner circuit, too. With her stepmother, she attended a gathering at the Connaught Hotel.

Raine was a busy little bee. She had just been appointed by her old friend, the Egyptian tycoon Mohamed al-Fayed, to the board of directors of Harrods and was about to attend her first meeting there. The lady who had once been Countess of Dartmouth and then Countess Spencer had wasted no time in marrying a third title after the death of Diana's father in 1992. Thirty-three days after she met Jean-François Pineton de Chambrun at a dinner party in April 1993, they were married.

Her appointment to Harrods was like a cheerful incentive, for she had, only a few days earlier, announced her divorce from the Gallic aristocrat. Raine would remain, however, the elegantly titled Countess de Chambrun, a bustling figure on the social scene, coiffed and bejeweled like a figure from a Fragonard cartoon. Her mother, Barbara Cartland, ever a study in the power of pink, continued to grind out her romances and say nice things about Diana to whomever would sit still for five minutes.

That day at the Connaught, the conversation turned briefly to Mohamed's son Emad (always called Dodi). He was in Los Angeles, officially setting up movie deals but really spending more time in pursuit of a playboy's life—squiring actresses and models and giving lavish and unruly parties in mansions he rented for a month or two and left in a state of disrepair. Supported by his father in his pursuit of the high life, Dodi—divorced for several years—coveted fame more than fortune: to be seen with a beautiful international celebrity meant everything to him. Would Diana not like to see him again? Raine asked. The Fayeds would be thrilled to arrange a dinner. But Diana was not interested in men who juggled simultaneous or even serial affairs, and that was the reputation of the younger Fayed.

Harrods, owned by Mohamed al-Fayed, a man several times denied British citizenship because of various business intrigues and tax problems, was itself the reason for the celebration that November day. The largest and most fashionable department store in the world, Harrods is patronized by the wealthiest and most famous residents of, and visitors to, London (and even by members of the Royal Family);

it is considered the jewel in the nation's commercial crown. Like Princess Diana herself, Harrods represents, in the popular consciousness, the best England has to offer even while it enjoys significant international cachet.

At this point, it is worthwhile to reflect on the world's endless fascination with England, for it is doubtful that Diana could have achieved her extraordinary stardom (or sustained it) had she not been a member of Britain's Royal Family.

Despite the waning of the Empire, England continues to enthrall, for it is one of the few countries that can boast an ancient past as well as a creative involvement in the present. At its best, England offers a long and illustrious history of great literature, not merely polite language; of admirable civility, not only cautious politeness; of the honor of tradition, not just empty mimicry.

Diana—born of the upper class—charmed millions not least because she mingled freely and effortlessly with all sorts of people. Hence she stood for the new classless society that all the world is supposed to see as the fruit of democracy. Her treatment of those on the margins of polite society—prisoners, the demented, those dying from AIDS and other diseases—her clear gaze and concern (coupled with her very unroyal custom of refusing to wear gloves to shake the hands of commoners) instantly endeared her to everyone. She looked wonderful in both formal gowns and casual slacks, in diamond tiaras and fisherman's caps, whether perfectly coiffed or with windblown hair.

In this regard, Diana more than any designer, model or movie star shifted the conventions of fashion in the late twentieth century. As royal fiancée and young princess, she was as much a victim of Buckingham Palace style as she was of their stale encrustations of decorum: a broad-brimmed hat, usually worn with a veil and gloves, was the order of most days. Accepting her mother's counsel on the appropriate way she should dress as the Princess of Wales in her early twenties, she wore nothing trendy, nothing chic, nothing sexy.

But around 1991, all that changed. *Harper's Bazaar* presented her in a daring creation by Gianni Versace, a powder blue dress of stretch fabric with gold studs on the side; this she so admired that she ordered several in other colors. Four years later, international houses were designing for her, and she made famous the work of British designers in London and on the continent: David and Elizabeth Emanuel and Catherine Walker (at their own London salons), John Galliano (heading Christian Dior), Alexander McQueen (at Givenchy) and Stella McCartney (at Chloé).

But by the end of her life, Diana had lost interest in fashion for its own sake, and in glamour as a value. "At first, everyone said I was the Marilyn Monroe of the 1980s, and I was adoring every minute of it. But this is an isolating experience, and the higher the media puts you, the bigger the drop. There are more important things in life than clothes, after all. There are people dying in the streets."

People mattered to her, not clothes—hence she turned inward and asked herself what sort of woman she was becoming, not what sort of clothes looked best. It was no accident that on more and more visits to hospitals at home and danger zones abroad, she wore a plain shirt and slacks, even blue jeans. With her royal ancestor Queen Alexandra, Diana could have said, "I know better than all the milliners and antiquarians what is best for me. I shall wear exactly what I like."

6

TRAVELING LIGHT

I hate nobody: I am in charity with all the world.

—JONATHAN SWIFT, *Polite Conversation*

December 1996—January 1997

The long holiday that is December began with a renewed annoyance: the media reports of Diana's infatuation for Hasnat Khan, the Pakistani heart surgeon. "She had become increasingly fond of Hasnat," said an unidentified friend to the press, "and by this time she was ever more impressed by him and attracted to him. Almost a year ago, she suddenly realized he might be the man for her, and their relationship had been developing ever since."

Unlike James Hewitt, who made a tidy sum of money by publicizing his affair with Diana, the doctor said nothing more than Diana did—that is to say, not a syllable; and in the absence of manifest evidence, it is impossible to know the extent of their "relationship." It is certainly possible that there was a brief affair: Diana was not immune to male seduction, and she was certainly capable of reducing a man to the condition of a smitten schoolboy on the spot.

Of some interest in understanding her heart's desire that winter is the fact that during 1996 she took an inordinate interest in cardiothoracic surgery—specifically, she went so far as to scrub up, pull on a surgical gown and watch a heart operation performed by Khan at Harefield Hospital. In addition, the opening of an international cardiac center brought her to Sydney. Dr. Khan also visited Kensington Palace at least twice, and Diana called on him frequently at his office and home, a few convenient steps from Brompton Hospital, which that same season had a greater claim on her volunteer time.

More important than the exact nature and extent of their intimacy—and unless Khan speaks, we shall never know—is the fact that Diana, as usual, plunged herself fully into sharing the interests of the men she respected. In this regard, she was no mad liberationist—as she was no iconoclastic republican eager for the collapse of the monarchy. Quite the contrary. In all these matters, Diana was very much a Spencer, very much raised in the traditions of the upper class. She differed, however, in her utter lack of snobbery and affectation, and in her abiding conviction that essentially we are all classless before God.

In any case, the press seemed not to care much about Dr. Khan after that spring; finally, he faded into the footnotes of Diana's history. As early as December 2, stories about him were reduced to page-four items, while the front page was reserved for Diana's campaign on behalf of Centrepoint, the London charity that looked after homeless children and teenagers and tried to rescue them from addiction, prostitution and all the worst effects of rejection.

Diana's concern for the homeless had a long history. Two years earlier, on a raw winter night, she had dropped into a shelter called Off the Streets, to visit forty prostitutes, addicts and alcoholics who had no homes. Moments before she arrived, an angry, disheveled young man said to Paul George, one of the social workers, "I think the

IRA should shoot all these royals. And when Diana comes in here, we can start with her!"

Moments later, the Princess arrived and, as George recalled, the angry troublemaker was the first man singled out by Diana. Hurrying to greet him, she extended a hand, smiled and said, "It's Ricky, isn't it? Didn't I meet you when you were sleeping down by the Strand?" She had, indeed, made several incognito visits to the sturdy London artery which connects the City to the West End. Here, vagrants with nowhere to go sleep under bridges and in alleys. On one occasion, she brought William and Harry to help dole out soup.

"That's right," said Ricky, beginning to melt in the warmth of her presence. "I'm getting myself together now. I'm really trying." There was no unpleasantness as Diana and Ricky chatted and she made certain there would be counseling and medical help for him.

"It's customary at this time of year," she said that December as holiday anthems sounded and the gift-giving season shifted into high gear, "to focus attention on those less fortunate than ourselves. Homelessness is not just a problem that miraculously appears on the first day of the Christmas season and disappears after. It is a perennial problem. If an Englishman's home is his castle, what happens to him when he has no home? And if that Englishman is young—perhaps mid-teens or early twenties—what greater risks will confront him?" As she wrote these remarks, she told a close friend, she could not help but think of her own two sons.

The boys were the center of attention on December 8, when Charles and Diana together attended a Christmas carol service in which William took part and, later, a play at Harry's school. "I had hoped to see Charles more content," Diana reported to a confidante, "but he seems sad. I have no bitterness. I'm not in love with him, but of course I love him as the father of my sons, and I admire his courage.

He has so much to go through with his family. I don't sit here with resentment—I sit here with sadness, because a marriage hasn't worked. But I also sit here with hope because there's a future ahead, a future for my husband, a future for myself and a future for the monarchy."

As for Camilla, Diana was brilliant: "She deserves a medal, that one," Diana said with absolute gravity. "What loyalty—really, who could doubt that she's the love of his life? She has stood by him during all this time and all this muddle. I hate it when people compare us and try to stir up all this hatred. Well, maybe once I was the worst offender. But all that's past now."

The morning of December 9, Diana addressed the Federation of Anti-Leprosy Associations in London—another disease whose victims she literally touched and embraced, thus shocking everyone. Leprosy (Hansen's disease) is not, as is commonly thought, contagious on contact, and so during a visit Diana was planning to Africa in January, she intended to convey a powerful message about the scourge of the disease as well as the relative ease with which it could be prevented and treated—but only if proper hygiene and appropriate medications were made available in afflicted countries. Embracing lepers was as important a sign of commitment as hugging those suffering from AIDS. She could not imagine not doing it.

From the speech, she hurried back to Kensington Palace, and from there sped, via Concorde, to New York for a gala ball benefiting the Costume Institute of the Metropolitan Museum of Art. Three thousand guests paid $125 each for the dinner and dance, with another nine hundred paying $1,000 each for the privilege of an introduction to the guest of honor.

Liz Tilberis, editor of *Harper's Bazaar*—with her white buzz cut and black sheath dress—might have stolen the limelight, but that, of

course, was trained uninterruptedly on Diana. Her entrance was heralded with a blast of silver trumpets and flashbulbs as she glided into
the party in a midnight blue frock by John Galliano of Dior that
looked like nothing so much as an opaque nightgown. Designed to be
worn without a bra, it made dancing awkward, and so Diana, plead-
ing exhaustion, left immediately after dinner and hastened to bed at
the Carlyle Hotel.

After a flurry of gift-buying and school parties in London, Diana
slipped out of Britain on Christmas Eve. Traveling with her assistant,
Victoria Mendham, in the economy section of a commercial British
Airways jet, she arrived on the island of Antigua and then proceeded
to Barbuda's plush K Club, a very private retreat owned by Aldo Pinto
and his wife, Mariuccia Mandelli, of the Italian fashion house Krizia.
There, in a luxurious suite priced at $2,700 per night, she remained
for a week, swimming, nursing a mild sunburn, having long phone
chats with William and Harry and seeing no one except Mendham.

The holiday had a subsequent unhappy development, for Diana
had presumed that Mendham would pay her own expenses: she had
done so on two previous holidays they shared. When the bills arrived
the following month and the young woman was handed a note detailing expenses totaling $6,000 each, an unpleasant conversation ensued
and Mendham forthwith resigned her position. This departure was
the fifth in fourteen months among Diana's staff, a crew of men and
women who observed a discreet silence with the press but who privately admitted that they found intolerable their employer's fierce
work schedule, the long hours, the uncovered expenses and virtual
complete submission to the Princess's erratic schedule. There is no
question that Diana was a demanding colleague, and she certainly
seems to have misunderstood the nature of employee expenses. There
was a $600,000 annual allotment for office and staff provided by her

divorce settlement, but with almost a dozen employees, such wasteful extravagance as she showed in relation to staff would have quickly depleted the funds.

On New Year's Day, Diana was back in London; hours earlier, Charles, William and Harry landed in Switzerland for a ski holiday.

The first Christmas after the divorce of the Prince and Princess of Wales had passed quietly. Indeed, the resentments and rancors of the past were fading as Charles and Diana focused on the needs of their boys. To the astonishment (and doubtless the disappointment) of some journalists, they were toning down what had come to be known as the War of the Waleses. Diana even spoke publicly of her affection and admiration for her former husband, and of her wish that nothing hinder his good relations with their sons. To that end, neither of them jostled for position in the boys' affections, and each was generous in encouraging the other to enjoy extra time with them.

The deep changes in Diana's attitudes were noted not only by her friends, but by the press, too. Gone was the nervous attitude of a woman surrounded by a small platoon of retainers and servants; absent, too, were the dozen pieces of baggage, the steamer trunks that invariably accompanied her journeys; most notably, there was a kind of directness, simplicity and serenity in her conversations, as if something had been freed in her. According to close friends like Rosa Monckton, this had less to do with the freedom of divorce and the satisfaction of every caprice than with a new commitment to finding her way through the thicket of sudden independence, which can be as daunting as any restriction on freedom. Diana had often spoken of her life as comparable to that of a soldier negotiating a journey through perilous wartime terrain laced with land mines. The danger, she knew, had not entirely passed, but at least she had charted it. One thing was clear: the life of mere glamour was not nearly enough for her. Her life needed substance.

The metaphor of a minefield was oddly appropriate that winter, for Diana had been struck by news from Amnesty International as well as the British Red Cross that one of the worst horrors of wartime was the hideous suffering and death caused by land mines. Determined to do something about this and to put on the line her commitment to humanitarian causes, she left London for Angola early on January 13. This African nation had been torn by twenty years of civil war and was littered with mines. One of every 334 inhabitants was an amputee as a result of an explosion, and everywhere the roads were full of limping children and deformed adults. Diana arrived to focus the attention of the world on this dreadful situation, and to bring pressure for an international ban on mines.

Until now, she had dedicated much of her time and effort to specific national causes, institutions and individuals. "I found myself more and more involved with people who were rejected from society," she had said; "with drug addicts, alcoholics, battered this, battered that— and I found an affinity there." A lonely child of a broken home, then a young woman with the highest expectations dashed in a marriage the world thought must be ideal in every way, Diana had known the most desperate kind of self-loathing and recrimination. Convinced that her loveless union was her fault, she punished herself; feeling unattractive and unwanted, she rejected her own body—hence the refusal to accept nourishment that is at the root of bulimia.

Beautiful clothes had covered her like costumes, makeup had provided masks, and her children her only validation. She had chosen lovers capriciously, and they were, to a man, not the sort to provide any kind of sustained emotional support. In this regard, she had been for years locked into a sort of repetition compulsion: she sought the cool, distant, otherwise preoccupied image of Charles in her lovers, as if by sheer force of will she could at last transform the experience of her husband—could, in other words, prove that one like him loved and embraced her.

The irony lay in the fact that precisely by picking emotionally unavailable men who were simply besotted with her beauty, charm and sexiness—not to say bedazzled by her status and position—she also selected exactly the men who would disappoint her. They were attractive, they were lithe and loving and even emotionally needy themselves. But they lacked the strength she needed, and their values were, in perhaps every case, not nearly as refined as hers. This led to a cycle of disappointment from which she might have emerged as a bitter, loveless woman.

There is perhaps no explanation for the fact that Diana Spencer did not become an emotionally wizened, suspicious, embittered woman whose inner potential vanished and whose outer charm turned to gelid manipulation. Perhaps it is only what we call grace that saved her from the results of her own excesses. The truth is that, for all her occasional blasts of silly recrimination (she lived to regret openly the television interview, aimed to hurt her husband and his family), Diana matured out of all proportion to the equipment she had and the experience meted to her. Stripped of her royal title, she wore the most majestic human quality of all—quiet, dutiful, responsible empathy toward those who suffer. With the ancient Queen Dido in Vergil's *Aeneid,* she could say, "I am no stranger to unhappiness, and so I have learned how to lend a hand to the needy." She acted not out of *noblesse oblige*—still less out of a desire for praise: she saw suffering and tried to heal it.

"In hospices, I found people at their most vulnerable, when they are dying. They are much more real than other people. And I saw that and appreciated it. They taught me so much. And when I sat there and held their hands, people were sort of shocked. But to me it was quite a natural thing to do. And when I saw the reassurance that an action like that gave, I did it everywhere and will always do so."

The most photographed human being in history, she never became accustomed to the press of cameras. But she learned, in her last year, to use this, too, as an opportunity—hence the trip to Angola that January. Checking into the British Embassy in Luanda for her four-day sojourn under the auspices of the Red Cross, she was without lady-in-waiting or secretary, without press officer or hairdresser. Accompanied only by her Kensington Palace aide Paul Burrel acting as baggage-handler and assistant, she refused the offer of first-class seating for the eleven-hour flight: "Wouldn't it be absurd," she asked the few international pressmen who greeted her, "to arrive in one of the world's poorest countries wrapped in a cocoon of luxury?"

Before nightfall on the thirteenth, sixty media representatives had heard of her trip and arrived, too—including a BBC crew of four, with whom she agreed to cooperate on a forty-minute documentary for the religious affairs program *Heart of the Matter*. This she permitted only because she was guaranteed that the film's proceeds would benefit the Red Cross, and that the content would concern not her but the cause at hand, the ban on land mines. "I hope that by working together in the next few days," she told the crew, "we shall focus world attention on this vital but, until now, largely neglected issue. So let's get on with it!"

Diana knew that she was visiting a very dangerous parcel of Africa. Mike Whitman, director general of the British Red Cross, escorted her for the journey across Angola. "She is aware of the risks," he said, adding later that from time to time she needed some reassurance. It is perhaps refreshing to see Diana as Whitman described her: occasionally wide-eyed with fear, as anyone would be, especially when a radio bulletin warned of a perilous area.

She would have been foolish to be imprudent, and in fact her visit was all the more admirable in light of the terror that gripped her several times. As she met score after score of amputees, the detachment of armed guards assigned to her side gave little optimism; she knew very well that danger attended every step. "There could be no more appropriate place to begin this campaign than Angola," said Diana as she visited victims at a modest orthopedic rehabilitation center in Luanda. Going from place to place in a dusty Range Rover, she wore nothing more elegant than flat shoes, sleeveless blouses and calf-length chinos or blue jeans or khakis and plain white shirts.

Diana and her friends might have expected a mixed reaction from some British politicians, but no one was prepared for the explosion detonated in London. A defense minister huffily called her "a loose cannon, ill-advised and unrealistic about foreign policy." To his credit, Prime Minister John Major hurried to defend her: "The Princess shares with the Government the common objective of trying to see an end to the use of land mines, particularly their indiscriminate use."

Informed of the controversy, Diana waved away objections: "This is a distraction we do not need," she said. "For some time I've been aware, through the Red Cross, of the continuing tragedy posed by anti-personnel land mines. But I wanted to do more than just read about statistics. My purpose is simple—to heighten global awareness of the human suffering caused by these evil weapons. I am only trying to help—to highlight problems going on all over the world."

Could any other reaction have come from a compassionate mother of two, faced with the dreadful human toll in a country with the highest death rate in the world and massive disability by weapons of war? She had no comment to the disapproval back home. Instead, she literally stretched out her arms to infants stunted by hunger, disease and disability; she knelt to hear the accounts of limbless soldiers; she brushed tears from the cheeks of teenage girls with terrible wounds to their faces. And she spoke with unhesitating passion about the statistics she gathered: twenty million active land mines still awaiting their victims; a dozen category A diseases raging through central Africa—Ebola, blackwater fever, cholera, typhoid—and minimal access to doctors and medications.

At a makeshift clinic, Diana leaned over an eight-year-old girl and asked what she would like. "A toy," whispered the child.

"What kind of toy would you like?"

"I don't know," said the girl, reaching for Diana's hand. "I don't know what toys are like, because I never had one."

"Diana is the Princess of Peace," said twenty-two-year-old Bernado Cupemula, a patient at the hospital in Huamba whose legs were missing. "I don't know who she was," said twenty-three-year-old Adriana Paulino, who had lost both legs and an arm. "I am just very happy that someone came to talk with me. People must know what is happening. This lady is making a difference." Nearby, Diana donned a flak jacket and visor to cross a path through a minefield.

On Thursday, January 16, she departed Angola, vowing to continue her crusade against the hideous weapons by traveling later to Bosnia, Cambodia and Afghanistan. "I have always wanted to travel like this," she said, "with very little baggage. I can have more contact with people this way, and there is less formality. It is the format I have been seeking for some time. I came as a Red Cross volunteer, not as a politician. I am not a political but a humanitarian figure—always have been, always will be."

She turned toward the plane that was to take her home. "I have never been anywhere like this, and I found it very humbling. You read the statistics, but actually coming here and seeing people struggling to have a life again after having limbs ripped off—it is shocking. I have lasting impressions of people trying, trying to rebuild their lives. It is all very touching." And how did she learn to cope with the sight of such suffering? "Every one of us needs comfort at some time in life, and for these people that time is now. If they can bear the suffering, I can endure the sight of it. They must not be left alone. I will be back here to see how they are doing. But if I'm to carry on with this anti-land mine issue, there are other countries I will need to visit, too."

It is important to stress that Diana was, that winter, giving her name and face to a cause that would otherwise have been the province of television producers and magazine editors. "Given the personality-crazed world we live in," wrote one American political commentator, "hers was an invaluable contribution." It became more so later in the year.

Lord Hurd, former Foreign Secretary and a confidant to Diana, recalled that she visited several times in 1997 to discuss her work abroad. "I think she discovered something about herself. It wasn't just that she was beautiful and famous. She had this gift which is some-times pompously called empathy. She put herself easily in other peo-ple's shoes, and all sorts of people found that she wanted to use her gift with people who were suffering."

David Tang, the Hong Kong tycoon who had planned a charity benefit in Diana's honor for the autumn of 1997, agreed. "There was an instant radiance when she walked into a room. At our first meet-ing, in London, she told me that she would accept our invitation to come to a Hong Kong AIDS hospice. 'I admire the work of hospices,' she said. 'Do you think it would be a good idea for someone like me to come and show that Britain has not forgotten Hong Kong?'"

"I'd like to be an ambassador for this country to every country in the world," Diana said during the last winter of her life. "I'd like to represent this country abroad in the best way possible—by showing the essential tolerance and concern that is the best of England, the best of any people." Hence she felt it necessary to know the most dedicated workers—physicians, scientists, organizers and volunteers for charities and fund-raisers—and to make them and their work a priority in her life. And as her circle changed, it was perhaps inevitable that some of her earlier friends would find themselves no longer part of that circle—the people who simply dined with her or skied with her or went to parties with her.

"Of course she enjoyed the glamour of her life," said Lord Hurd. "But this wasn't sufficient for her. All the reports of her visits abroad emphasized the glitter of it all. But she was always looking for ways she could use that to the good." And so her visits to places like Angola, where it was impossible to find anything at all pretty or appealing.

Diana's charm was, of course, a quality immediately mentioned and often critiqued by those who met her. In an age obsessed with fame, when many people depend on their connections (however distant or tenuous) to celebrities in order to invest their lives with glamour or even with meaning, Diana was the object of attention and desire. World leaders from Mitterrand to Mandela were won over by her, and a few journalists, like Alan Hamilton, who frequently followed her on press junkets, recalled that often there were surprises. Bored to distraction by a protracted state banquet in Lisbon, she reverted to a schoolgirl's mischief: the Portuguese president, Mario Soares, was wearing bright red suspenders, and Diana, with an earnest, straight-faced glance, leaned over and snapped them loudly.

On another occasion, the Amir of Qatar subverted every convention and invited Diana to sit at his side for a state dinner—normally a strictly male event in the Islamic world. This broke a tradition and, since that time, women in important positions have been moving to the head tables not only in Qatar but in other formerly restricted Islamic venues.

Hence as 1997 began, Diana—freed from the pressures of the Foreign Office and liberated from court protocol—finally found her place in a world far larger than that in which she had been raised or into which she had married. The polite life of the titled aristocracy, the remote life of the Royal Family—all of this paled into significance. Forlorn in her early experiences with her own family and forsaken by her adopted one, Diana found the truth at last. In a way, her lovers had provided only the beginnings, only the catalysts, and they could neither prevent her from involvement in a larger world nor, after all, satisfy the deepest cravings within her. If she had not been crushed by disappointment, she would not be derailed by romantic illusions.

Whereas she had once been England's shy rose, virginal and uncertain, now she learned to accept the touch of devotion and to give it in almost limitless response. Her own heart had been wounded by deep sorrow, but she had passed through the frontiers of remorse and into clearer fields. Unafraid at last, she pitched herself into the world of the poor—a universe of its own that she saw bereft of compassionate love, its inhabitants longing for the embrace of those, like herself, who had not forgotten them.

7

TO THE LIGHTHOUSE

For Mercy has a human heart,
Pity a human face,
And Love, the human form divine,
And Peace, the human dress.

—B L A K E , *Songs of Innocence*

February—May 1997

While Diana and the shattered people of Angola were stinging the conscience of Britain through the BBC documentary, televised on February 11, an entirely different kind of publicity was being generated by Sarah, Duchess of York.

Fergie, divorced from Prince Andrew, had accumulated over $7 million in debt—mostly from an apparently psychotic need to shop, she said—and her former mother-in-law refused to bail her out. Quick to realize the value of her position and connections, the Duchess signed to write an autobiography *(My Story)* and even to make television commercials for Ocean Spray cranberry juice and—in light of the fact that she had shed some excess pounds—for Weight Watchers.

Her publicity machine cranked up, not with glamour but with glitter, in February as she accepted an invitation from a Viennese construction magnate named Richard Lugner to endorse his latest project. Paid $40,000 simply for showing up, Fergie arrived at an Austrian shopping mall, signed copies of her autobiography, attended an opera ball and departed in a whirl of giggles, winks and slightly racy humor. "Quite simply, the Duchess of York is a vulgarian," sniffed the legendary courtier Lord Charteris, former secretary to the Queen and one of her closest confidants. "She is vulgar, vulgar, vulgar and that is that." His Lordship was not known for cryptic opinions.

"Fergie is very much in the rent-a-royal business," said British journalist Brian Hoey, referring to the Duchess's willingness to hire herself out for personal appearances at a sizable fee. "She really is her own worst enemy, whereas Diana appears not to be able to do a thing wrong." With a small staff helping her to arrange her own schedule, Diana never gave any thought to engaging a media representative. Fergie, on the other hand, hired Howard Rubenstein, a New York public relations wizard, and signed with International Creative Management to handle her literary affairs and her commercial interests. Her divorce settlement from Prince Andrew provided just under $3 million, but $2.1 million of that went into a trust fund for her daughters, the Princesses Beatrice and Eugenie.

Her first life preserver was the contract to write her memoirs, published in November 1996 with a color jacket photo of a barefoot Fergie—an unsubtle reminder of the infamous foot-kissing episode with former lover John Bryan. Predictably, the book was a huge success in America and England, although not so successful as to add more to her coffers than the $3.7 million advance Simon & Schuster doled out. But another $3 million came from her television commercials, Austrian print ads in which she posed using Olympus cameras, interviews with *Paris-Match* and so forth. She paid her debts—but not her tax bill, which came to $2.7 million. More commercials were on the way by the autumn of 1997—and, more to the point, the inevitably unfavorable comparisons with the good and kind Princess of Wales, whose humanitarian efforts were tireless.

Of course, Diana did consort occasionally with the merely fashionable sector of society, and her friendship with designer Gianni Versace was much in the news in February. An admirer and a wearer of his clothes, Diana had agreed to contribute a foreword for his book, *Rock and Royalty;* her fee and a substantial portion of the book's royalties were designated for AIDS research.

But on February 10, there was some embarrassment—which could have been avoided if Diana had shown a bit less faith in Versace's publicists and a bit more foresight about the wayward antics of editors who prepare illustrated books about fashionable designers. The finished album, to her chagrin, featured quaint photographs of Royal Family members alternating with provocative shots of semi-nude male models and athletes grinning like idiots or, conversely, wearing that blank, stony-faced anger that passes for urban chic. There was, for example, an old photo of the Duke and Duchess of Windsor juxtaposed with a picture of a near-naked Ryan Giggs, the Manchester athlete. A few pages later, there was a portrait of a man with both hands stuffed into his underpants—and nearby, a snapshot of the Queen. Bare-chested young men in leather abounded, as they had in Versace's previous book, *Men Without Ties,* who, in some cases, were also without anything else.

"I am extremely concerned that the book may cause offense to members of the Royal Family," said Diana. "For this reason I have asked for my foreword to be withdrawn from the book, and I will not attend the dinner on February 18, which is intended to mark the book's launch." At once, Versace prudently canceled the gala dinner, refunded $400,000 worth of tickets and promised an equivalent donation to Elton John's AIDS Foundation. So ended an episode of body-baring followed by face-saving.

Ironically, as if on cue, Diana then attended the charity premiere of Richard Attenborough's new film, *In Love and War,* on February 12; the story focused on the quiet heroics of the Red Cross. As a curtain-raiser, an edited version of the BBC documentary recording Diana's visit to Angola under the auspices of the Red Cross was screened. This elicited from Attenborough a memorable comment as he publicly thanked Diana: "For someone described [by a minister of the previous government] as a loose cannon, she has scored one hell of a bull's-eye." The evening raised over £100,000 for the Red Cross campaign.

That evening, Attenborough saw what he considered a prime example of Diana's kindness and goodwill. His seven-year-old grand-daughter Lucy had practiced her curtsy to Diana all day, but when summoned to hand the Princess a bouquet and a program, the child forgot to curtsy. "When I told Diana that Lucy was mortified, she immediately turned back from the threshold of the auditorium and asked to be shown the curtsy. 'I've never seen a more perfect one,' she said." Nor, it might be added, was any princess more deserving of such a bow in homage.

Ian Kelly, one of the actors in *In Love and War,* spent twenty minutes with Diana that evening. His recollections are fascinating.

"It seemed very right that the film was rather upstaged that February evening not only by Diana herself—with a catlike grace, in a slinky blue sheath—but also by her television documentary on the land mines of Angola, which preceded the film.

"She seemed very relaxed, towering above Attenborough and Chris O'Donnell [the film's male star]. One was immediately struck by her physicality, the way she moved, the extraordinary vitality of the woman—even more so later, close up. She looked in control, like a dancer or an athlete. The evening proceeded as these things do: crowds and flashbulbs outside the cinema, a crush to get to The Savoy for the Red Cross dinner for 500 afterward. Once there, Diana laughed loudly and frequently. I noticed her swap earrings with Chris O'Donnell's mother.

"It was then that Attenborough motioned to me to meet the Princess at his table. After introducing us, he went off table-hopping, leaving me for twenty minutes with the most famous woman in the world.

"She turned her attention on me like a spotlight, but without much eye contact at first. It was her quality of listening that was remarkable. We got off to a bad start: she understandably assumed that I had worked with Attenborough frequently before and that I was American, because I had played one in the film. When I corrected her on both counts, she said with a laugh, 'Oh, *good!*' She spoke of Richard, how much she 'adored and admired' him. 'We've known each other forever—all through my Strange Existence,' she said, paraphrasing, with knowing irony, *Evita*.

"In the film, I played a Red Cross volunteer disfigured by burns who later commits suicide, and Diana knew the burns unit where I had researched my role. She spoke of how much she had loved the film and, kindly, my brief performance.

"She was fascinating—much cleverer and more articulate than I had supposed she would be, informed and thoughtful in particular on disfigurement and what such people present to the world. I joked how, as a redhead, I often get to die in films or plays and never get the girl. She laughed. 'Harry's hair is ginger, of course, but it's best to say strawberry blond, don't you think?'

" 'Like Robert Redford.' "

" 'Exactly.' "

"She spoke of her boys with all the luminous love of the best mother—and, like every mother, she knew they would leave her. 'They're mad for girls, of course,' she said. 'William asked me to buy six Valentine's cards for him to send—*six!*—and I'll be lucky if one of them is for me.' "

"We talked of land mines—it was the serious subject of a dazzling evening—and she talked of how she got involved and the who-approaches-whom of the royal endorsement of projects. And then, with great politeness, she said, 'I think we need to talk to Richard [Attenborough] about seeing more of you in his next film.' "

" 'Absolutely, ma'am. I want no prosthetic scars—and I want to get the girl!' "

" 'But redheads don't, do they?' she said, her eyes twinkling. "

" 'No, ma'am.' "

"Attenborough was back, hovering. I was about to leave then, and suddenly, somehow, I became all formal. 'It's been an honor meeting you, ma'am.' "

"She smiled—the way a girl does when you've just ruined a date with one asinine line. I had put the wall back up, but one of us had to. Better it was I."

Much of the rest of February was devoted to the press release and general planning for a major event to be held in June in New York City. One evening that winter at Kensington Palace, after discussing her new life with her elder son, Diana told him that she had too many expensive clothes and that she preferred a scaled-down life and a simpler wardrobe. Well, said the canny young prince, why didn't she auction them off and give the money to charity? Millions could be raised and her own goals achieved easily, quickly and to great effect.

Next day, after a few telephone calls to Christie's chairman, Diana got the auction house to agree to offer eighty of her gowns and dresses. In signed documents, every penny of profit was destined for the AIDS Crisis Trust and the Royal Marsden Hospital's Cancer Fund in London, and (in America) the Harvard AIDS Institute and the Evelyn H. Lauder Breast Cancer Center at Memorial-Sloan Kettering. "I am extremely happy," said Diana, "that we can raise money this way for important charities. Yes, of course it is a wrench to let go of these beautiful dresses. But I am extremely happy that others can now share the joy that I had wearing them."

Most of the items, designed by Victor Edelstein, Zandra Rhodes, Norman Hartnell, Bruce Oldfield, David Sassoon, David and Elizabeth Emanuel and Catherine Walker, were a perfect fit for the five-foot-ten-inch, American-size 6 or 8 wearer. Soon, Christie's published 170 catalogs autographed by Diana (on sale at $2,000) and another 5,250 (unsigned) at $265. And with that, opined *People* magazine even as it mixed metaphors, Diana "shed part of her rudderless past and put a spin on the future."

As for herself: "Life has moved into new and exciting areas. Clothes are now not as essential to my work as they used to be." Still, the catalog revealed the range of clothes that could be taken as markers in the growth of their owner: first, the frills and satins of a fairy-tale princess, then the sleek designs of a mod glamour girl, finally, a sophisticated, concerned ambassador.

Most poignant of all—and a fact not known to most people at the time—was that Diana's favorite designer, Catherine Walker, had been diagnosed with breast cancer in 1995. "I have received unfailing support from the Princess since that time," said Walker, "and I am therefore deeply moved that my designs, through the Princess, are now being used to save lives."

As it happened, the event raised even more money after Diana successfully sued *The Express on Sunday* after the newspaper falsely claimed that she would keep some of the proceeds from the auction. The paper was forced to pay £100,000 libel damages to one of her favorite charities, the Royal Marsden Cancer Research Fund.

Despite the divorces of the Waleses and the Yorks and of Princess Anne and Captain Mark Phillips (and Anne's subsequent second marriage, to Commander Timothy Laurence, one of the Queen's equerries), the limelight remained focused on Charles and Diana—or, more accurately, on Diana only. Charles's more and more open relationship with Camilla—and his hosting of her fiftieth birthday party in July 1997—made few headlines, as if it were expected, hence boring, lacking significance. And even the resolute bachelorhood of the Queen's youngest child, thirty-three-year-old Prince Edward (long rumored to be quietly gay) failed to generate much interest.

But nothing Diana did or said was unimportant; even something that did *not* happen was newsworthy—as, for example, her trip to Southeast Asia. According to the terms of her divorce, Diana was required to obtain the approval of the Foreign Office for any journeys outside Britain that were not a simple private holiday. She had readily been given leave for the trip to Angola and for the charity events in America, but her request to further her anti–land mine campaign in Cambodia was deemed too dangerous, and permission was denied.

"It is simply not safe," said a senior officer. "We would say the same about any place in that region where the Khmer Rouge operates. They don't respect boundaries. Her safety is all-important, and there are other places in the world where she could bring the issue to attention that would be more sensible." In addition, there was some fear that a visit to Cambodia would interfere with Britain's efforts to free Chris Howes, the British mine-clearance expert being held by the Khmer Rouge.

Another sort of danger zone had been safely negotiated, however. On March 9, Diana and Charles were photographed together in the presence of the Queen for the first time since 1993. The occasion was an official family photo marking the confirmation of Prince William at St. George's Chapel, Windsor—a venue separate from that of his classmates, for William did not wish the presence of his family to upstage the occasion for others.

At a luncheon at Windsor Castle following the ceremony, William's parents chatted amiably, to everyone's relief—most of all, it can be imagined, the Queen's. She was so pleased at the lack of family tension that she urged on the guests and godparents for the taking of the group picture, "Come on, move forward or you won't be in focus. You see, I *do* know something about photography!" This would not be considered riotously funny from anyone else, but the press considered it a triumph of spontaneous, witty understatement from Her Majesty.

On March 15, Diana departed for a four-day visit to her brother in South Africa. While she was there, President Mandela heard of her private stay and at once wanted to transform her visit into a semi-state function. Posing with Diana for photographers, he praised her work in Angola and on behalf of AIDS patients. "If I can do anything to help in any way," she said, "I will be available to do it."

Mandela's mention of Angola was carried further by the London press on the nineteenth, when Diana was back in London. At a Savoy Hotel luncheon, she presented a medal for bravery to Chris Moon, the thirty-three-year-old former land mine clearer who lost most of his right leg and a hand to mines in Mozambique. "The evidence of his courage," said Diana, "is before the eyes of all in this room. Chris Moon truly symbolizes what selfless bravery is."

On Easter Monday, the last day of March, Diana requested an analogous act of bravery from a stranger, in an incident that must rank as one of the most bizarre and poorly understood little melodramas of her life.

At ten-thirty that morning, Diana left the Earls Court Gym on Earls Court Road—a place she occasionally visited for a workout, as she did the Chelsea Harbour Club and a Kensington hotel gym. On departing the gym, Diana was photographed by Brendan Beirne, a thirty-nine-year-old well known to her, since his specialty was casual snapshots of the royals.

"She was walking down the street looking quite happy," said Beirne later. "I took a couple of pictures of her and thought that was it. I was about fifty feet away, on the other side of the street, and I put the camera down for a moment. Suddenly she saw me and ran across the road, saying, 'What are you doing? What are you doing? Give me the film!' "

Precisely at that moment, a twenty-eight-year-old stranger named Kevin Duggan passed by and was enlisted by the Princess to assist her. Duggan pinned Beirne to a wall and Beirne claimed Duggan threatened to break his arm. All the while, Diana continued to scream, "Get the film! Get the film!" This, indeed, she did herself, quickly removing the film from Beirne's camera.

"It was outrageous," said Beirne later. "She knows I am neither a stalker nor a threat. I have taken photos of her for ten years! But she is very manipulative. She can shout at photographers, but then the next day she is tipping off someone so they know where she is and comes out smiling."

The police, once they heard the account, were disappointed in their favorite princess. "This is no way for the Princess to behave," said an official. "Even if she is fed up with the paparazzi, she should have protected Beirne from the extreme reaction of Duggan."

But the reason for this severe reaction may have been revealed later when Diana kept her luncheon date with a forty-one-year-old bachelor friend, property developer Christopher Whalley, whom she had met at the Chelsea Harbour Club. There were, as it turned out, widespread whispers that Diana's reaction to Beirne's camera being trained on her had to do with the fact that she feared being seen having lunch with Whalley. Of their relationship, nothing can be known for certain, although they were at last caught by a photographer, lunching again in London on May 26.

On the morning of April 8, rejecting the usual trappings of royal travel, Diana paid cash for three tickets at Victoria Station and took her sons aboard the train to Gatwick Airport. From there they took a British Airways flight to Antigua and, as has become her custom, they proceeded to The K Club on Barbuda. By month's end, they had returned, the boys were back in school and Diana was keeping a restrained schedule and, as the press noted, a low profile.

At the time of her death, journalists and media commentators had the proverbial field day tracing the trajectory of Diana's long, tangled relationship with the press. Sometimes attentive, often brash, theirs had indeed been a mutually rewarding and jointly suspicious liaison; it would not be excessive, in fact, to compare them to lovers grown complacent.

For perhaps a decade or more, Diana's concept of herself was formed through the lens of the press: through the media's reflection, she saw who she was, who she could become, what the public liked about her and how she was progressing. But from the time of her separation in December 1992, there was a marked shift. As Diana found her own voice and asserted herself, she no longer merely depended on the press—she tried to control it, and this was, ultimately, the Faustian bargain that went wrong, for her goal was, of course, an impossible one.

Remarkably, by the summer of 1997 there was what one acquaintance, Sally Quinn of *The Washington Post*, called "an incredible sense of irony about herself, her image and her publicity. She didn't seem at all angry about the press. On the contrary, she was what I would call accepting. I asked her how she withstood the lack of privacy and the unbelievable media interest in her. She smiled and shrugged and said something to the effect of 'what will be will be.'" With that, Quinn felt that Diana "had actually discovered who she really was."

Diana kept mostly a quiet agenda in the spring of 1997, visiting hospitals two or three afternoons a week and, just as often, but without the risk of being photographed, at night. Long weary of the formal rituals of royal charitable involvement, she was acknowledged by everyone to have a genius for comforting those in distress. In addition, she occasionally brought her sons to the world of the sick and the maimed and the dying. Death did not frighten her, she said, and she wanted to assure that fear of it would not exert power over William and Harry.

There were, of course, the predictable objections to this aspect of her sons' education, but Diana was quick to counter. "Am I doing them a favor if I hide suffering and unpleasantness from them until the last possible minute? The last minutes which I choose for them may be too late."

As Richard Attenborough recalled after Diana's death, no subject more occupied Diana's thoughts and conversation than her sons. He had the clear impression that she longed to give them the most normal life possible while simultaneously preparing William for accession to the throne. But, he added, she believed with all her strength "that many of the old conventions had to be blown away, that her children should be allowed to witness the life led by millions of United Kingdom citizens.

"She knew how to make a real connection, enabling people to talk to her from their hearts about what really mattered," said Christopher Spence, president of the London Lighthouse. He recalled that it was Diana's manner as well as her words that drew people to her: climbing onto a patient's bed or crouching beside a wheelchair or reaching out to touch or hug, she fixed her eyes on someone and asked, "Hello—how are *you?*" and the person became, for that moment, all the world.

"She was always real and spontaneous," Spence continued, "without any agenda, formula or need of protocol. She never rushed or left anyone out, and she could make even brief moments seem spacious." Diana's last visit to the Lighthouse was in June, on the day of a particularly nasty onslaught against her by the press. Putting aside her own hurt and anxiety, she went from patient to patient as if nothing were bothering her. "This morning I arrived in a filthy mood," she told Spence as she departed, "but I'm leaving on top of the world."

But parallel with the continued dedication to the sick and the outcast, there was a curious strain in Diana's life from the time of her divorce in the summer of 1996 to late spring 1997. Several members of her staff (including her private secretary, two assistants and a driver) resigned, disappointed in her moody attitudes toward them, her suspicions that they were leaking details of her private life to the press, and her unpredictable expectations of their working hours. Diana had been so rejected by the Windsors that she saw everyone connected to them as her enemy—including Tiggy Legge-Bourke, who had long been her sons' nanny and was now more of a guardian to William and Harry as they balanced school life with shuttles to and from Charles and Diana.

An attractive, attentive, thirty-one-year-old woman, Tiggy had coped, a year earlier, with the completely unfounded rumor that she had aborted Prince Charles's love child. This was not the only trauma in Tiggy's life at the time. Jealous of her sons' affection for Tiggy and unreasonably fearful—as her own life seemed to become more and more isolated—that she would be left alone to wither in Kensington Palace, Diana made life difficult for both Tiggy and the boys (not to say her staff) when she fixated on the governess that spring. It was a difficult time in the Princess's life—as had been the autumn of 1995, when, also "at her worst" (as Rosa Monckton said), Diana took to television to proclaim her victimhood.

This bruise in her nature is, of course, easy to understand: she had been abandoned by her mother, her husband, her in-laws, the very institution of crown and country she had been raised to venerate, and so it would have been natural for her to fear for her relationship with her sons, too. Her insecurities were bred from hard experience: they were not neurotic fantasies without foundation.

Diana spent the entire day of May 1 at the Trinity Hospice in Clapham, South London; there she visited patients suffering terminal cancer and the latter stages of AIDS. "The visit made a lot of people very happy," said Annette Moore, a patient who was battling advanced cancer. "It was a boost for all of us. She listened more than she spoke."

When she had something important to say, however, Diana spoke up without fear, false humility or hesitation. So it was, when a few days later, she went to the Roehampton Priory, an expensive private clinic for those suffering from emotional or mental illness and those recovering from alcohol or drug dependency. When she visited places like The Priory, Diana was pleased to share details of her own past problems—her bulimia, for example—for she wanted to encourage others to triumph against what sometimes seemed terrific odds. It was always made clear, however, that what she said in her sessions with patients must remain confidential.

Her angry disappointment was understandable, then, after details Diana had confided to a group at The Priory were given to the press by a member of that group with an eating disorder. *The Daily Mail* published the details of Diana's experience, including her allegations that her bulimia was due to the loneliness of her royal life and the dissolution of her marriage; she also said that she always feared suffering a relapse.

For openers, the newspaper told how Diana began to suffer bulimia as a teenager, when she saw her sister Sarah become anorexic. "I never really understood why two sisters would develop such similar diseases, but we did." The condition, Diana added, was aggravated by her isolation from reality and the coldness she felt from the Windsors. "It wasn't great, that environment I had with my husband at Balmoral or Sandringham. I was so unhappy when I went back there that the bulimia just got [worse and worse]. It was a situation in which nobody ever treated me kindly."

She had suffered no relapses since 1994, Diana said. "But like many an addiction, it can come back one day to haunt you. It will always be in the back of my head. I could go back to it, but I don't want to. I channel my energy into other things." She had, she admitted, spent thousands and thousands with psychiatrists, but she found that experience "pointless, because the people trying to help me hadn't been through what I had been through. In some cases, I ended up thinking it was they who needed help, not me." She added that The Priory was much the best way—joining professional help to group support: "I think someone who has been through a similar situation is much more able to give advice than someone who has not."

Her remarks—disappointed though she was when they were circulated—reveal a remarkably self-aware and sensitive woman. "You have to address this anger that's inside you," she told the patients. "There's anger towards your loved ones, like your parents and your husbands who don't understand your anxieties. An eating disorder is not about fitting into a small dress. It's in the head. Anorexics have a tremendous amount of anger because you are slimming to such a degree and it isn't what you wanted to do in the first place. As for me, I suddenly awoke one day and thought, 'I've had enough of everyone treating me like absolute rubbish—I must stick up for myself.' Everyone knows how to treat you when you're vulnerable, but if you show any sign of strength, it is they who end up feeling intimidated."

Diana concluded her remarks by describing her survival strategy: exercise, times with good friends and a sensible eating plan in which she constantly reminded herself what she needed to eat for good health.

This did not mean, however, that she had no insecurities, or that every emotional problem had been resolved; indeed, she remained one of the most insecure adults her friends knew. According to her close friend Rosa Monckton, "She was so incredibly insecure, and whenever people got close she got very frightened. That's why she lived her life in so many tight compartments. She didn't introduce her friends very often. You know she was just so scared of losing people or of people rejecting her."

That month, Diana's insecurities may well have suggested to her that confidences were being broken left and right: her mother, Frances Shand Kydd, granted an interview to the pictorial *Hello!* magazine in which she discussed her own past. Now divorced, a convert to Roman Catholicism and living in virtually monastic isolation on an island off the coast of Scotland, Frances spoke quietly but frankly about the breakup of her unhappy marriage to Johnnie Spencer—and this, she felt, foreshadowed Diana's own heartache and disappointment. Diana's wedding, she said, was not real happiness but rather "a mirage of happiness." Her daughter did not appreciate the reading of her mind, especially since at the time of her marriage to Charles there were no confidences exchanged between mother and daughter. But this interview did not, as some reported, cause a permanent rift, and several times over the summer Diana enjoyed long telephone conversations with her mother.

On May 22, Diana traveled to Lahore, Pakistan, for a two-day campaign to raise money for a cancer hospital for the poor. This she did for her friends, the Englishwoman Jemima Khan (daughter of the recently deceased tycoon Sir James Goldsmith) and her husband, the athlete Imran Khan, now also a politician. They were rebuilding the bombed hospital with funds raised from international parties.

Arriving at the Lahore airport, Diana was asked by a reporter if she was pleased with the Pakistani government's ban on land mines. "Yes, I am," she replied, continuing on her way.

But the reporter pressed her. "Can you say anything more than yes?" Diana turned to him with a grin and said, "No."

Next day, she toured the hospital, which had been partly destroyed by a bomb the month before, and after visiting the patients and staff, Diana pledged to sponsor a fund-raiser in London. Her cherished memento from this hospital visit was a photo of herself cradling a dying child. "This little boy is now dead," she said months later. "I had foreseen his imminent death before taking him in my arms. I remember his face, his pain, his voice. This photo is very dear to me. It's a private moment in public circumstances."

It was, in fact, one of the experiences that changed her that year; in the midst of so much hurry, of such media attention and so many compliments, the mystery of death surrounded her so often that no values went unquestioned, no presumptions about what constituted a life of meaning and substance went unexamined.

That afternoon, she slipped off for tea with Dr. Hasnat Khan's parents (no relation to Imran), who also lived in Lahore—and at once the press read this as confirmation that not only love was in the air but also imminent marriage to the London-based heart surgeon.

Diana had chosen to visit Pakistan without an official police escort, so the comedy of errors and misunderstanding was not, of course, clarified by an intelligence officer who said of Diana's trip, "We had no idea where she was. We were looking everywhere but had totally lost her." The officers, assigned to protect the Princess from possible terrorist activities, were themselves almost paralyzed with fear—at least for their jobs—when they learned that one of Imran Khan's cars had been used to transport Diana to her teatime engagement and back to Jemima's home.

To make matters worse (or, for the media, more exciting), Hasnat's aunt Ghasia said later that day, "Oh, my nephew and the Princess are in the throes of an Eastern love affair" (whatever that was). And from America, Hasnat's cousin, Naeem Kham Tareen, weighed in: "She wants to marry Hasnat. They are in love."

This romantic spin was then denied by Hasnat's mother, Naheed: "She is a friend and she respects his work. There is no romance. Hasnat has never expressed any wish to marry Diana, and she has never expressed any wish to marry him." Hasnat's father, Rasheed, a retired colonel, added that the couple was incompatible in any case—not because of religious background but because "my son is a doctor, and she is a social worker. She likes ailing humanity. Because of that, they are friends—but I don't think they will be married."

That turned out to be prophetic, but at the time the silence of Kensington Palace added to the general confusion and speculation: in a triumph of ungrammatical obfuscation, a spokesman told *The Daily Mail*, "Who the Princess wishes to see during her visit is her own business."

And that was the end of the two Khan visits and, it seems, of any relationship with the surgeon.

8

AFLOAT

With everything that pretty is,
My lady, sweet, arise.

—SHAKESPEARE, *Cymbeline*

June—July 1997

On June 12, Diana addressed the meeting of an anti—land mine campaign in London and discussed her visit to Angola the previous January.

"How," she asked, "can countries which manufacture and trade in those weapons square their consciences with such human devastation? Suffice to say that when you look at the mangled bodies of some of the children caught by these mines, you marvel at their survival. Even if the world decided tomorrow to ban these weapons, this terrible legacy of mines already in the earth would continue to plague the poor nations of the globe. In my mind a central question remains: should we not do more to quicken the de-miners' work, to help the injured back to some sort of life, to further our own contribution to aid and development?"

Whereas earlier there had been some resentment about Diana's outspoken campaign—some politicians having called her involvement shortsighted—now the reaction was unanimous. The consensus was reflected in a remark by Bruce Kent, the former general secretary of the Campaign for Nuclear Disarmament and an active opponent of land mines: the Princess should not be afraid to dabble in politics, he said. "Everything is about political values. You don't change anything if you don't change political structures."

The issue of land mines was paramount in her next long journey, too, when the normally cool socialites of Washington and New York, once again and to no one's surprise, fell adoringly for the Princess of Wales in June.

In 1985, Diana and Prince Charles, then the golden couple, had swept into the capital and jubilant crowds had cheered everywhere they went, as if for the arrival of rock stars. Indeed, not since the Beatles had landed in New York two decades earlier had their been so wild a reception for a British contingent. But there was a difference. The hysteria of 1964 was for a quartet of pop singers, and in 1985, it was for the so-called fairy tale couple—and everyone knew, particularly her reserved husband, that it was actually for the glamorous Princess. A dozen years and numerous visits to the capital later, what had once been called Di-mania had not lessened one atom.

On Monday evening, June 16, 1997, Diana attended the eightieth birthday celebration for Katharine Graham, where, in a simple black pantsuit, she chatted easily with three Supreme Court justices, two senators, various congressmen, magazine publishers and Georgetown socialites. Graham asked Diana about her journey to Angola and the talk of Diana going to Bosnia; the Princess was, said the respected newspaper and magazine publisher, obviously very brave indeed. "But I don't want to talk about these things," Diana told Graham, "unless I really go to the places where they're happening and see them for myself." Similarly, later that summer Diana told her friend Rosa Monckton, "I want to walk into a room, be it a hospice for the dying or a hospital for sick children, and feel that I am needed. I want to do, not just to be."

The important work began the next day at an outdoor news conference, where Diana could not have been more direct. Speaking with barely concealed anger that alternated with grief, she addressed the subject:

"The years of civil war in Angola have left behind a deadly legacy of 15 million mines scattered around a country with a population of 10 million. I met children who have suffered the most horrendous injuries, having stepped on mines which lay hidden in the grass around their villages—which resulted in many having their legs or arms amputated. As they grow up, these children may need to have continuous operations as bones grow through the skin of amputated limbs. They may also become a burden to their own families, as most will have difficulty in making a living and may well be seen as social outcasts because of their disability. Having seen for myself the devastation that anti-personnel land mines cause, I am committed to supporting in whatever way I can the international campaign to outlaw these dreadful weapons."

Elizabeth Dole joined the Princess in calling for a ban: "If this were taking place in Alabama, not Afghanistan, or in California, not Cambodia, what we are about would not be an admirable cause, it would be an urgent crisis."

That evening, Diana attended a benefit dinner for the Red Cross, where 400 guests came to see and smile at their famous guest, radiant in a red beaded dress, her blond hair swept casually back. But the evening was not, as they say, "about glamour." From her perch between

Elizabeth Dole (American Red Cross president) and John Kerr, the British ambassador, Diana rose to address the crowd at the National Museum of Women in the Arts.

The event raised $600,000 for prosthetic devices and rehabilitation programs, but there was a bitter irony in Diana's presence in Washington. The United States consistently (and as late as the autumn of 1997) blocked efforts for an international ban on land mines. As the largest producer of such weapons, America also argued for a continued use of mines in demilitarized zones—on the border separating North from South Korea, for example. Diana was not unaware of the position taken by her host country that June.

Although the trip was considered a private visit by Buckingham Palace and the British Embassy, Diana's agenda in Washington also included a breakfast meeting with the First Lady and a stop at Bethesda Naval Hospital, where Diana met with a Brazilian soldier who had lost a foot during his mission to remove land mines from the Honduran-Nicaraguan border.

She also slipped off to the children's ward of a hospital in a poor section of Washington, where a very ill child of eight asked if she could visit the palace in London. "Oh," said Diana, lifting the girl up on her knee, "you wouldn't like it—it's a very stuffy place." Moments later, she astonished one of the nurses by asking about her young daughter, Ericka Alston, who, when Diana had visited three years earlier, was ill with cancer. As it happened, Ericka had since died; Diana extended her visit to spend time with the still grieving mother. "She remembered everything about my little girl," said Gayle Alston. "I don't know how she did it. Then I learned that many others had the same experience. She remembered. People mattered to her." Which is why, one might add, she mattered so much to people. The designation "Queen of Hearts" was not an empty cliché.

From there, Diana hurried back for a few days in London, where she hastily arranged to spend time with William and Harry. But even so simple an event as a day with her boys could be riddled with outlandish difficulties. On June 22, without knowing the political implications of the film and of her attendance at it, she took William and Harry to see *The Devil's Own,* starring Brad Pitt and Harrison Ford. But the movie, according to some critics, appealed to pro–Irish Republican Army sentiment, and this set off an angry skirmish in the London tabloids.

"I didn't know what it was about when I took them," Diana told magazine editor Tina Brown the next day in New York; nevertheless, she had to make a public apology for "any distress which may have been caused" by the outing. "We just wanted to see a movie," she added in her talk with Brown, "and we picked it out because William likes Harrison Ford. I issued a statement right away, and I called Prince Charles and left a message. I didn't want him to think I was deliberately making trouble." Apparently her detractors, who took the matter with such gravity, failed to recall the wise saying of Alfred Hitchcock, "It's only a movie!"

Next morning, Diana was back on the Concorde to New York, where she visited Mother Teresa at her AIDS hospice in a depressed area of the Bronx. "She is a remarkable woman, in love with the poor and their plight," said the frail, eighty-seven-year-old nun who had first met Diana half a dozen years before. "I regard her like a daughter, and I am always glad to welcome her to our homes for the sick." There they were, the most unlikely of partners—fair, tanned Diana, tall and stately at five-feet-ten-inches plus high heels, holding hands with dark and weathered Mother Teresa, barely four-feet-eleven-inches tall and unsteady after several heart attacks.

They clung to each other for a moment; they spoke of the land mine crisis, of the hopeful but still uncertain new treatments for AIDS patients and most of all of the hard, earnest love that working with the poor and dying must always entail. Diana promised to visit Mother Teresa in Calcutta later that year and then departed the mission, clutching rosary beads the nun had given her as a modest memento.

She was, Diana told her friend Rosa Monckton, almost speechless with admiration: a simple little Macedonian woman had, in less than fifty years, made an enormous difference for millions of the world's suffering people. Now, as her life drew to a close, Mother Teresa, who had been awarded the Nobel Peace Prize in 1979, could look proudly upon the order she founded: it now counted 5,000 nuns and brothers operating more than 2,500 orphanages, clinics and hospices in over 120 countries. Neither sanctimonious nor judgmental, the nun saw and accepted the complex conundrums of Diana's life. And it was true: Mother Teresa loved her like a daughter.

From one of the poorer parts of New York, Diana was whisked south to the Four Seasons restaurant on East Fifty-second Street for lunch with Tina Brown (editor of *The New Yorker*) and Anna Wintour (editor of *Vogue*). That evening, there was a glittering party on Park Avenue, where, at a preview prior to the auction of her gowns at Christie's, she chatted amiably with the guests—among them Henry Kissinger, Patty Hearst, Kate Moss and Barbara Walters. She departed New York the next day.

On June 25, seventy-nine of her dresses and gowns brought in $3.26 million. The off-the-shoulder, ink-blue velvet dinner dress Diana wore the night she danced with John Travolta at the White House sold for $222,500; a pearl-embroidered white sheath with matching jacket (which Diana called her "Elvis dress," and which she wore on a state visit to Hong Kong and to film premieres) went for $151,000; a one-shouldered, draped cream silk chiffon with translucent gold glass beads brought in $75,100.

And so it went, the average sale price of the items going for more than $41,000. "Diana Cleans Out Her Closet," ran a page-one headline in *The New York Times,* "and Charities Just Clean Up." But Diana Spencer Windsor was cleaning out more than her wardrobe: she was, in fact, completely altering the spirit of her life. As she had said, "Life has moved into new and exciting areas. Clothes are now not as essential to my work as they used to be." Friends used the words "liberated" and "unfettered" to describe Diana in the late spring and summer of 1997—as if the once beleaguered, wretchedly unhappy Princess, who had for so long been the envy of so many, had been sprung free from a lunatic asylum or from captive enslavement by terrorists.

"She's living her life as she wants to live it," said Rosa Monckton, adding, in a clear reference to the Royal Family, "and she's free of the restrictions she had before. You can see that in the way she looks. She's much happier with herself, and she's more calm. And, as for the charity work she wants to do, she's much more hands-on. She'd much rather go to the heart of it than be dressed up at a film premiere."

At the time, few people knew that Diana was godmother to Domenica, the daughter of Monckton and her husband, *Sunday Telegraph* editor Dominic Lawson. The child, who has Down's syndrome, was often and lovingly visited by Diana, who became very active in the appropriate charity. "Diana spends time with children in the intensive care units of hospitals. She wants to help, so she's out there, learning and listening and doing."

But these reports did not entirely capture the spirit of Diana. Part of her was restless to find exactly what she was in transition *to:* charity work was a consuming passion, but Diana was not about to join Mother Teresa's community of nuns. In other words, she wanted very much to use her fame and her influence for the good of others, but she also had a private life to think of—and this had to mean more than being a goodwill ambassador or guiding her sons through the thickets of adolescence.

There had to be a life *for herself*—but just how she would find that was uncertain. "The first word that enters the mind is 'lonely,' " said a close friend. "It's a big change when you suddenly move out of one life and enter another one." A new life, for Diana, meant remarriage, or at least something analogous to what her former husband enjoyed by this time: a stable, serious, long-term relationship.

Charles and Camilla were both divorced, hence no longer adulterers, and now they were being seen more and more openly in public. He was even planning to honor Camilla's fiftieth birthday at a lavish party at Highgrove, and there was talk of a gradual acceptance of her by the public. Early that summer, in fact, a documentary on the Prince's inamorata was shown on English television, and there was considerable speculation that this heralded the beginning of her debut as the Prince's consort.

A few days later, on July 1, Diana marked her thirty-sixth birthday, and, by happy coincidence, her brother Charles, now a resident of South Africa, was in town. Along with 550 others, he attended a gala centenary fund-raising celebration—a dinner-dance at which Diana was guest of honor—at the Tate Gallery. All this was detailed by the press, but a private luncheon three days later was not.

Shortly thereafter, Diana and Princes William and Harry had a private meeting with Prime Minister Tony Blair and his family at the Blairs' official country residence, Chequers. Although the matters at hand were never officially disclosed, Diana did confide in Tina Brown: "I think at last I will have someone who will know how to *use* me. He's told me he wants me to go on some missions." A position as a roving ambassador for charitable causes was something she much desired and to which Blair was committed: he saw not only her influence for good but also the value of her politically neutral voice. Neither of them had any desire to compromise her position as a former member of the Royal Family; and neither of them wished to exploit her enduring relation to that family as the mother of the heir to the throne.

On July 11, Diana sailed into the deep and heady waters of controversy as she took her sons on holiday with her to the South of France. They were the guests of Mohamed al-Fayed, the owner of (among other important properties) Harrods department store in London, the Ritz Hotel in Paris and the Paris estate of the late Duke and Duchess of Windsor. Fayed, a friend of Johnnie Spencer, had known Diana since her childhood.

He had an eight-acre holiday compound near St. Tropez, and nearby he docked his schooner *Sakara* and his impressive, 190-foot yacht, the *Jonikal*, which was equipped with saunas, a gymnasium and a helicopter landing pad. A spokesman for Harrods told the press, "Mr. Fayed and Diana, Princess of Wales, are happy to confirm that they and their families are having a private holiday together."

The controversy was at once clear. Under the terms of her divorce, Diana could not leave the country with her sons without the explicit permission of the Queen. The press immediately began to murmur that such leave could not possibly have been given if it were known to Her Majesty that the host was Fayed: he had consistently failed in his bid for British citizenship after the Department of Trade and Industry questioned his business dealings and credibility. Regarded in Britain as the vulgar, *arriviste* Egyptian and briber of Members of Parliament, Fayed was the object of considerable slander among the English—and most particularly among both aristocrats and royals. "Like me," he said of Diana, "she has been persecuted by the establishment." In Fayed's favor, however, it must be said that the government's case against him has always seemed, to some, manufactured—and perhaps based on a resentment that an Egyptian family had taken over that most cherished institution, Harrods.

Diana's presence among Fayed's guests, therefore, was considered inappropriate at best and downright traitorous at worst—which may or may not have been among her complex of motives. For the moment, however, the presence of the young Princes (not to say Diana's popularity) forestalled any official denunciation. Besides, Prince Charles's imminent celebration of Camilla's birthday hardly gave the press or the palace a mandate to question the propriety of Diana's holiday with her sons and an old friend of her father who was clearly a paternal and not a romantic figure. Still, photographers pursued Diana and the boys everywhere. Shots of them on jet skis or swimming began to appear in newspapers and magazines around the world—primarily because Diana looked spectacular in a swimsuit with a faux leopard-skin design: her avid gymnasium training had produced appealing results.

On July 14, to the grateful surprise of an international crew of photographers and reporters, Diana motored out in the water to greet them and their long lenses. Begging for privacy, she gave them an opportunity to click away to their hearts' content for a few moments—and then she made an enigmatic little speech: "My sons are always urging me to live abroad and to be less in the public eye. Maybe that is what I should do, given the fact that you won't leave me alone. I understand I have a role to play, but I have to be protective of my boys. William gets very distressed, and he can get freaked out by all the attention. But you are all going to get a big surprise with the next thing I do"—which, it was reported, she said with a touch of both whimsy and bitterness.

If Diana indeed promised a "big surprise" (and if those words were not merely a photojournalist's fantasy), then it may have been her intention to announce her departure from England to live elsewhere. But after calm reflection and discussions with her sons, she publicly disavowed the statement the next day.

"In the light of reports in this morning's newspapers," ran a press release from Kensington Palace, "Diana, Princess of Wales, wishes to make clear that she did not give any exclusive interviews to reporters yesterday. Her purpose in talking to some journalists was merely to inquire how long they intended to remain in France, as the oppressive media presence was causing great distress to all the children. There was no discussion of the possibility of any statement being issued in the future."

Diana may well have realized she had spoken to the press precipitously—that her relocation outside Britain would mean limited access to William and Harry, over whose travels the Queen had direct control. An indication of this logic may be inferred from her words to a reporter from the Paris newspaper *Le Monde* a few days before her death: "Any sane person would have left England long ago. But I cannot. I have my sons."

The next day, July 15, Diana learned about the murder of Gianni Versace outside his Florida home. They had enjoyed a cordial acquaintanceship when they met for designs and fittings, and the news was, of course, very much upsetting. This was the dangerous extreme of celebrity, she told friends by telephone. Who could foretell what lunatic might attack her or one of her sons? For several days, she was not easy to spot in the St. Tropez harbor, on the Fayed speedboats, or on the beaches of her host's villa. Her retreat from public view was variously ascribed to the party at Highgrove for Camilla (on the eighteenth) and to distress over Versace's death.

But on July 19, the glamorous Diana—who now, it seems, wore little other than a swimsuit during her entire holiday—was photographed being cooled down, doused with a water hose by an unidentified teenage girl. Despite her attempts to get the media to leave her family and friends alone, they continued to be stalked. The paparazzi also trained their telephoto lenses on her swinging merrily on a rope from the yacht *Jonikal* into the sea; a snapshot sold for $50,000.

Looking tanned, relaxed and cheerful, Diana and her boys arrived in London on July 20 aboard Mohamed al-Fayed's private Harrods airplane. That evening, she kissed William and Harry, promising that they would be reunited after their holiday with their father at Balmoral and before they returned to school in September. But this was the last time they would ever see her.

The next day, Diana was at Northwick Park Hospital, near Harrow, Northwest London, where she cuddled a four-year-old child (named Camilla) who was suffering the ravages of cancer and had lost her hair because of chemotherapy treatments.

That same evening, traveling on Elton John's private jet, Diana departed London for the Versace funeral, held in Milan on the twenty-second. Wearing a single strand of pearls and a classic black Versace dress, she was photographed seated with Elton, in the family pew with the Versaces. He and Sting joined their voices in the motet of the twenty-third Psalm, but for much of the service, Diana had to comfort John, who often burst into sobs.

On July 27, Diana was back in London—just in time to hear Prime Minister Tony Blair speak supportively of her and her former husband:

"I think it is very important that Princess Diana is allowed to carry on the work that she is doing. She earns a lot of respect and admiration from people all around the world. I'm very happy for that to continue. She has done an immense amount for the causes she supports—as has the Prince of Wales. Of course, there are difficult human situations involved, but that shouldn't blight the fact that they both do a lot of work that gains respect around the world. I think the rest of the world sometimes wonders why they get pulled to pieces so much over here, because it is not very constructive. It is important that we recognize that they are human beings as well as people who occupy positions in the public eye.

"I do think it is important that the monarchy survives. When these key decisions need to be made [about Charles and Camilla?], I, as Prime Minister, will do what I believe is in the best interest of the monarchy and the country."

The very busy month of July ended as Diana again boarded the Harrods jet to fly from London to Nice, where she began a six-day cruise around the islands of Corsica and Sardinia. But this time, the circumstances of her renewed holiday were very different indeed.

9

ANOTHER COUNTRY

Beauty may captivate the sense,
But kindness only gains the heart.

—HENRY PURCELL, *The Fairy Queen*

August 1997

During July, a great deal had changed for Diana. Feeling, perhaps for the first time in her life, that she could assert herself without family repercussions and delighted to have an extended holiday with her sons before they joined Charles in Scotland, she ignored the snobbish reactions to her consorting with Mohamed al-Fayed's family. She swam and exercised, rode in speedboats, took her sons to beach resorts, met the press informally when it suited her mood and ignored them when she was weary of them. Healthy, sleek, buoyed by her friends and adored by her sons, she seemed to have it all.

There was even more. Diana seems to have fallen in love—or at least to have succumbed to a fervid infatuation, which was often the consequence of her passionate, impetuous personality. "I am a Cancerian to my fingertips," she had once said, referring to her earnest, emotional and vulnerable nature, her susceptibility to the blandishments of love, her fondness for the seaside and her ardor for a home life with a husband and children. And exactly two weeks after her birthday on July 1, the great final shift in that emotional life occurred in the entrance of Mohamed al-Fayed's son.

Emad Mohamed al-Fayed—always called by his nickname Dodi—was born in Alexandria, Egypt, in 1956 to Mohamed al-Fayed and his wife, Samira, sister of the arms dealer Adnan Khashoggi. During Dodi's childhood and before his father became a billionaire, Mohamed directed his brother-in-law's furniture import company in Riyadh, Saudi Arabia. The Fayeds divorced when Dodi was a child, and thereafter he attended schools in Egypt and Switzerland before graduating from the Royal Military Academy at Sandhurst. Afterward, he received a commission in the air force of the United Arab Emirates. His mother, Samira al-Fayed, whom he loved and admired, died in 1986.

But just as his father's tangled world of high business and finance intrigued him not at all, so was Dodi indifferent to a martial career. Instead, he set up a production company, Allied Stars, which invested in *Chariots of Fire, The World According to Garp, F/X* and *Hook.* He was never a creative contributor, and he demonstrated no particular commitment to the craft of film other than the desire to earn money from participation.

In 1987, he married the American model Suzanne Gregard, whom he divorced eight months later and to whom he gave (with, as usual, help from his father) a settlement of almost $2 million. "He was so romantic and thoughtful," said Gregard. "And he didn't take things too seriously. Once, during a candlelit dinner he had arranged, the table we were sitting at collapsed, and the whole turkey fell to the floor. We laughed so hard. That was what I loved about him." Yes, well, but . . .

"I think my one marriage has put me off the institution for life," said Dodi not long after. His major pursuit from that time was not even success in the movie business: he was forever in advanced training as an international playboy and charter member of the jet set. Like Prince Alexis Mdivani, Prince Aly Khan and Porfirio Rubirosa before him, Dodi amassed airplanes, houses, polo trophies and beautiful women. Aly Khan and Rubirosa were killed in auto crashes in Paris; Alexis died the same way—in Spain, while rushing to catch a train to Paris.

Darkly handsome, with gray-blue eyes, alluringly accented English and a chivalrously seductive demeanor, Dodi was romantically linked with a number of attractive and vivacious women— among many others, Princess Stephanie of Monaco; the actresses Brooke Shields, Britt Ekland, Daryl Hannah and Patsy Kensit; Frank Sinatra's daughter Tina; the singer Lindsey de Paul; and the models Marie Helvin and Kelly Fisher. Of this professionally diffident yet amorously busy man, one might say (altering the famous remark of Will Rogers) that he seems never to have met a woman he didn't like. But in fairness it must be added that he never had a reputation as a cad, much less as an exploiter of women. His partners were always willing mates and never had a bad word to say about their attractive escort.

"He will shower a girl with presents and talk all sorts of nonsense," said a friend to the press that month. "He's very keen on having bodyguards and likes to point out boats or buildings and tell people that they are full of his bodyguards. Dodi likes to be terribly sweet and caring and secretive with women, although his arrogance can come through once he's had a few drinks. He is the textbook playboy, the classic son of a very rich and powerful man." He was, according to *The Washington Post,* "a Hollywood dabbler who lived to get him-self in the gossip columns." Dodi al-Fayed, in other words, wanted very much to be taken seriously. But there was little reason for any-one to do that.

He was at every stage of life supported by the generosity of his father—to the extent, reported the press, of $100,000 monthly as spending money. The actress Claudia Christian, long a friend of Dodi, recalled that he "was always generous picking up the tab, but when it came to real money, the reins were pulled by his father. He was still a little boy."

In addition, Dodi had unrestricted access to Papa's array of prop-erties, which included a castle and 40,000 acres in the Scottish High-lands, a chalet in Switzerland and residences in New York, Dubai and Italy. The option of rented homes in Los Angeles was no longer avail-able to him after he was sued at least ten times by landlords who claimed that he reneged on monthly rents as high as $30,000 for a mansion that needed major restoration after his lavish, wild parties and sudden abandonment of the premises. As for transportation, he had several Ferraris, a 1928 Rolls-Royce Phantom One, a Sikorski heli-copter, a Gulfstream jet and unlimited use of Papa's $27 million yacht.

Dodi al-Fayed first met Diana in 1987 when Harrods polo team challenged Prince Charles's at Windsor. Dodi and the Princess then met occasionally but casually over the years, with little more than a polite exchange. But when Mohamed was host to the divorced Diana and her sons in St. Tropez in July, Dodi decided to join them. No one was prepared for what occurred on the *Jonikal,* least of all Mohamed. In his wildest dreams of a successful union for his son and sweet retal-iation against a country he loved, but which did not love him, he could not have imagined that the young woman he had known and regarded fondly since she was eight might fall in love with Dodi.

And so Dodi courted Diana with the fervent encouragement of Mohamed, who, of course, would have had many reasons to be proud to have Diana as his daughter-in-law, not least of which would have been the ultimate revenge against the Queen: the mother of the future king of England would be a Fayed. Beginning that July 15, a summer friendship blazed into an intense affair Diana later called the best intimacy of her life. "It is bliss," she told Rosa Monckton in a happy, confiding telephone call.

At first, Diana and Dodi could risk stepping out together, as they did when they met in Paris for dinner at the Lucas Carton restaurant on July 25; she was en route home from the Versace funeral. From the restaurant, they were close to the Ritz Hotel (also owned by Mohamed al-Fayed) and to the former home of the Duke and Duchess of Windsor (a mini-chateau also among Mohamed's possessions), and so they slipped away for time alone in the City of Lights.

The first week of August, the couple cruised the Mediterranean aboard the *Jonikal,* stopping at Corsica and Sardinia for swimming, leisurely walks and seaside suppers. Dodi had been known only to the most devoted followers of the tabloids; now, by virtue of his gradual emergence as the romantic partner of the world's most famous woman, he found himself exactly where he had never managed to be—at the top of the dubious world of international celebrity. It was this, according to friends and business colleagues, that he coveted even more than wealth.

On the other hand, nothing seemed to matter to Diana except her new love. Her affair with Dodi marked her first public excursion alone with a man who was not her husband, and—also for the first time—she neither denied anything nor attempted to flee its consequences. Perhaps she identified with the rejection Fayed felt from the Royal Family and its courtiers, who saw to it that he would never be a British citizen; perhaps, too, Diana was attracted to a dynasty that might help replace and fulfill the one she had just left.

And then, of course, there was the sheer glowing chemistry that bonded ardent lovers. A photographer with a long lens captured Diana and Dodi embracing, and this was the shot seen round the world—evidence at last, it was presumed, that Diana was involved in a serious romance. As it happened, the presumption was correct.

And, as perhaps expected, Barbara Cartland weighed in with an acute opinion: "Yes, Dodi ought to be an Englishman [for the sake of Diana's children], but we know perfectly well that she's been with an Englishman and it was terrible. They've ignored Diana. I don't think it should be any of their business [i.e., the people at Buckingham Palace]."

Furthermore, it was reported that Diana's sons liked Dodi, but it cannot be known how much they simply rejoiced in their mother's happiness and considered negligible their own feelings in the matter. As for Prince Charles, any eventual remarriage of Diana would, to be sure, make his life much easier. "I'm happy if she's happy," he said in an unguarded moment with a reporter.

After the week's lazy idyll aboard ship, Dodi and Diana took off for London on August 7. Wearing a clinging blue dress and looking burnished with sun and happiness, she popped in on a few friends before joining her lover at his Park Lane penthouse for dinner, whence she departed at one in the morning. The only wrinkle in the couple's undiluted pleasure was the report of an angry claim by the American model Kelly Fisher: she announced to the world that she had accepted Dodi's offer of marriage, had considered herself duly engaged, and now intended to sue for breach of promise and severe emotional distress. That action was eventually short-circuited by tragedy.

On August 8, Diana's bustling life maintained high speed as she departed for Bosnia and the continuation of her campaign against land mines. It ought to be noted that, even if someone had tried to dissuade her to subordinate a cause to her newfound romance, this seems not to have occurred to her as a real option.

For three days and nights, Diana (leaving Dodi behind) toured some of the most ravaged sections of Bosnia. Her hosts were two Americans, Jerry White and Ken Rutherford, founders of the Land Mine Survivors Network. White lost a leg when he stepped on a mine while camping with friends on the Golan Heights; in a similar accident, Rutherford lost his right leg and part of his left foot in Somalia, where he was doing relief work. With Diana, they traveled up and down the dirt roads into the towns and hamlets of the country.

"She used those remarkable eyes of hers to make contact with everyone," said White, "and she had an incredible humor to put people at ease." Rutherford agreed: "Everyone had an idea that she would act in a certain royal way, and she delighted in turning that upside down." In Tuzla, for example, Diana visited a Croatian man who had lost both legs and most of his eyesight in a land mine accident; then she met twenty victims whose plight was exacerbated by a fierce lack of daily necessities. And in another town, she met young widows, orphaned children and more of the wounded. In each case, the contacts were as moving for her as for those she comforted.

At one point, Diana and her hosts were in a school gymnasium with amputees trying to play a makeshift volleyball game even though they were limited to sitting or crawling on the floor. There was an awkward moment, and then White and Rutherford asked if Diana preferred to leave. With a smile, she replied, "Don't worry, boys—leave it to me." And with that, she went over to the wounded players, sat down on the floor with them, asked their names, shook hands with each and joined in their game.

On the same journey, Diana brought together two lads from opposite sides of Bosnia's ethnic partition—Zdravko Beric, a twelve-year-old Serb, and fourteen-year-old Malik Bradoric, a Muslim. Both boys had lost their legs in mine explosions. "I went to the woods to play," said Zdravko, "and while I was playing, I found an antitank mine, and it exploded." Malik was severely wounded while he was helping his father collect food from a relief convoy. In village after village, Diana embraced the maimed and the poor.

At the same time, Prince Charles was on a brief holiday on the Spanish island of Majorca. On August 9, his Mercedes limousine had a misadventure, careening down a tortuous road and barely avoiding a serious accident. He returned to his hotel shaken and upset.

Diana returned to London the evening of August 11, and next morning she sent a letter to White and Rutherford from Kensington Palace: "I was enormously impressed by the genuineness of your approach to the survivors and their families," she concluded, "and by your efforts to sustain their morale and to help them to maintain their self-esteem. Please keep me informed of all your activities and know that I shall continue to do all I can—and I hope to see you all again soon." She signed the letter, "With love from Diana" and added an "X"—thus sending a kiss to all those she regarded as new friends in such painful circumstances.

The people of Bosnia felt the genuine concern of the Princess of Wales, as did Mother Teresa, who said of Diana, "She had great love for the poor and a great desire to help and know more about them. She had the disposition of one who could have come to work with us."

Next evening, August 12, Dodi came to fetch her—again, in the now ubiquitous Harrods helicopter—and they whirled north to the village of Lower Pilsley in Derbyshire for a meeting with Diana's psychic counselor, Rita Rogers. The reason for the journey was not metaphysical speculation but friendly concern, for Rogers's companion was suffering from cancer. Their visit lasted little more than an hour, and although no details of the conversations were forthcoming, Rogers was known to dispense comforting encouragement rather than severe warnings. In any case, Diana had certainly ceased to predicate her life or her major decisions on a psychic or an astrologer. Rogers's estimations might be thrown into the mix of motives toward a decision about the possibility of marriage, for example, but Diana made the final choice.

On the thirteenth, Diana and Dodi briefly separated. He went to Los Angeles on prospective movie business (and, according to some friends, to scout a Malibu beach house as a possible occasional retreat for him and his new love). Two days later, she went to the Greek islands with her friend Rosa Monckton, but before they departed for Athens aboard the Harrods jet, Diana telephoned to chat with her sons, now at Balmoral with their father and the Royal Family. She missed them, she said, and longed to see them after their respective vacations—on Sunday, August 31, she promised.

No one was as loyal to Diana as Rosa Monckton, and none was so aware of her thoughts and feelings. Traveling together that last time, Rosa saw for herself the long reach of the press. Alone, hundreds of miles from the center of things, they sat in a small tea shop on the isle of Hydra when a passerby pulled out a tiny camera. "We'll be fine," Rosa told her friend. "It's only a tourist." Diana knew better: "We'll be all over the front pages tomorrow." And so they were.

With a captain and a crew of three, they cruised through the isles for five days, mostly unmolested by the press who had great difficulty locating them. Diana was grateful for the time to be, as she said, "just

Diana"—which meant no fussing with hair, no makeup, no designer clothes. Of their years of friendship, Monckton remembered most of all Diana's laughter, her sense of fun. Diana was an irrepressible mimic. One day she tried to get through to Prince William at Balmoral, but he was out. When Diana rang off, she turned to Rosa and, affecting a wickedly accurate Scottish brogue, imitated the castle operator: "Och, there goes the Princess of Wales on yet another sunshine cruise." Diana's gallery of characters was dead right and hilarious: friends, statesmen, courtiers—even the Queen. It was reported that she could have been a comic actress of the first rank.

According to Monckton, Diana saw a complete distinction between her personal life and her public duty, although she was as frail and vulnerable as the rest of us—in fact, rather more so. "She had a huge capacity for unhappiness, which is why she responded so well to the suffering face of humanity, and this was in no way alleviated by the glitz and glamour of her public persona."

Diana was, Monckton insisted, tireless in her ability to give to others and to put people at ease, which is, after all, the infallible sign of real royalty. "Completely unsnobbish and unstuffy, she never stood on ceremony or hid her warm personality behind her title. She was utterly devoid of arrogance, either natural or acquired." Most of all, Diana ignored her own comfort and schedule if a friend was in need. "When I lost a baby after six months of pregnancy," continued Monckton, "she, more than anyone, knew what to say and what to do. She was both compassionate and practical. These two qualities coexisted in her in a way I have never seen in anyone else. She instinctively found the words to ease the pain."

Diana passed the precious days in Greece with Rosa Monckton discussing many things of importance to her: Dodi, the nature and depth of their romance and what it might or might not portend, the future of her sons and her work on behalf of the world's forgotten. Few people understood how trapped she felt, according to Monckton, "and how much she craved an independence that most of us take for granted." Perhaps for that reason, "she had not made any decisions about her future." Such was also the opinion of other friends in whom Diana confided during those last weeks: the relationship with Dodi was "bliss," as she told Rosa, but at the last, she had very few illusions about life.

Diana needed to consider just how serious he was, just how serious *she* was—as well as her children, her future residences, her work. "Whatever happens to me in this relationship," Diana told Rosa, "I will continue to do my work, and to help where I am needed." As Diana told London columnist Taki Theodoracopulos that same month, "I haven't taken such a long time to get out of one poor marriage in order to get into another one." She understood men well, and she certainly knew Dodi's reputation. "If you have been rejected by your mother and then rejected by your husband," said Rosa Monckton, "and at the same time your receive this massive public adoration, you feel that as soon as people get to know you, they will reject you."

This new relationship, if it were to go anywhere, required considerable time. Nor was Diana going to play right into the hands of the Royal Family and alienate herself from her country, its people—and, by extension, her place in the lives of her sons. And Rosa remembered Diana saying, with absolute gravity, that her charitable works would in fact be even more important to her, because "the world Dodi inhabits is so far removed from reality." Rosa was not on holiday with a capricious woman about to make a foolish decision. As for Dodi's lavish gifts, Diana protested that they made her uneasy. "I don't want to be bought. I have everything I want. I just want someone to be there for me, to make me feel safe and secure."

D I A N A

On Sunday, August 17, the two friends docked on the Greek mainland at a small village called Kipazissi, and together—at Diana's suggestion—they climbed to the Orthodox Church. "So we went and lit candles for our children," said Rosa. Although Diana was not a conventionally religious person, Monckton insisted that she was indeed a profoundly spiritual one. On Diana's desk at Kensington Palace was a statue of Christ, and around it she had placed rosaries given to her by Pope John Paul II and Mother Teresa. In Diana's own hand on the desk was the motto: "You can't comfort the afflicted without afflicting the comfortable."

Rosa loved Diana because she was nothing like a plaster saint: she asked for advice, rarely took it, found criticism difficult and finally admitted her mistakes. Above all, she had a remarkable gift for empathy and for friendship. "I loved being with you and sharing so many important moments," Diana wrote to Rosa after the cruise. "True friendships are hugely valuable. We've stuck together through hell and back."

On August 20, the cruise was over, and Diana and Rosa were back in London. Dodi was there to greet them, and he and Diana left the next day for the Riviera, cruising from St. Tropez to Portofino, where they dropped anchor on the twenty-fourth; from there, the *Jonikal* sailed along, hugging the coast of the Italian Riviera—past Chiavari, through the azure blue waters off Sestri Levante, farther still past Monterosso al Mare. They arrived in the tiny Bay of Poets, between Portovenere and the island of Palmaria on the twenty-fifth. So far on this journey there had been only a few photojournalists in sight, and they had gotten some unremarkable shots of Dodi and Diana from afar. Finally, the couple landed on Sardinia. Their only companions were a small crew, the sun and the flying fish.

Prince Charles's Scottish holiday with William and Harry was drawing to a close, and before the boys returned to school it had been agreed, via telephone calls, that they would have at least a day or two with Diana in London. On Friday, August 29, she rang to tell the boys that she would be there late Sunday morning—and yes, they could meet her at the airport.

With that, Dodi suggested one last romantic summer night in Paris before their temporary separation. They would, he said, stay at the mansion his father now owned, once inhabited by the Duke and Duchess of Windsor—or perhaps in the Imperial Suite at the Ritz Hotel—or maybe at his apartment near the Arc de Triomphe—or maybe at all of these. Calls from Dodi and Mohamed and their staffs ordered everything to be prepared at all these places. It was all very luxurious and very royal and very impressive—and very, very perilous.

The summer had been frantic, Diana's schedule packed with virtually continuous activity. She had gone from airplane to helicopter to yacht, from schooner to airplane to limousine and back again to yacht, from limousine to helicopter to hotel to yacht and from war-torn country to lavish villa, from luxury suite to Kensington Palace, from lecture halls to seaside resort. Anyone attempting to draw up an hour-by-hour diary for the Princess of Wales would be confused by a calendar that was almost demented.

Alas, now things were getting out of control. Freedom was heady, independence was bending toward dizziness.

For a couple who were lovers, Diana and Dodi were, perhaps alarmingly, constantly on the move. Here now, later there; rushing from shore to shore, island to beach, city to country, hardly ever at rest—racing from one spot to another, hiding not so much from the press but perhaps from the questions they ought to have put to themselves.

What was their life going to be? What would happen when they went home—and what was home? Where could they be comfortable, at peace, and under what circumstances? They were on a treadmill to oblivion—going, always going. But was there an inward journey?

Who, indeed, *was* Emad "Dodi" al-Fayed? What was he *doing* with his life? What responsibility did he show toward others, or, more to the point, toward himself? He resented his father's benevolent tyranny, he disliked his reliance on his father's money and name and possessions. But what was he doing to establish a beachhead in himself?

How would Diana take to a man like this? How could a woman moved to tears by the plight of limbless children, of AIDS sufferers, of abandoned children, of battered wives, of homeless waifs—how could this woman pursue causes so urgent in our times when her lover's most serious concerns seemed to be the next cruise, the scheduling of a jet to whisk them to a spa, the time of the next party, the next distraction? This woman who felt so comfortable with Mother Teresa and with cancer-stricken babies—for how long could she sustain life as perpetual amusement?

The Diana so deeply loved by friends like Rosa Monckton was not a shallow denizen of the night. But she could make alarmingly bad judgments when it came to a choice of partner.

Her spirit was soaring—she was in love and she could, for perhaps the first time in her life, do what she willed—but in a way she did not know what that involved—what exactly *was* it that she willed? In some poignant ways, this sympathetic woman was still a child, thirty-six approaching nineteen, still fascinated by the Krazy Kars at the theme parks. When the pace and tenor of life quickened, her pulse did, too.

As August 1997 drew to a close, things were indeed out of control.

At 7:30 on Friday evening, August 29, the anchored *Jonikal* floated gently a few hundred yards offshore in the clear waters of a bay in northeast Sardinia. Dodi and Diana had slipped quietly onto a beach of the Costa Smeralda, the famously breathtaking Emerald Coast. The sea glistened in the late summer sunlight, Diana swam— her every move within the vigilant gaze of a Fayed bodyguard— while Dodi chatted in Arabic with an elderly Moroccan who rented boats and jet skis.

As the sky reddened, then turned metallic blue, the lovers retreated to the Cala di Volpe Hotel for a drink, where a few Italian photographers recognized them. It was high season for celebrities on the Costa Smeralda, after all, and at once there were men shouting and cameras shooting. Five minutes later, Diana and Dodi were back aboard the *Jonikal*.

The following afternoon, Saturday the thirtieth at 12:30, they climbed into the back of a white Mercedes belonging to Tomas Muzzu, a sixty-nine-year-old local who ran a taxi service for celebrities. Diana wore a beige trouser suit, Dodi black trousers and jacket with a blue T-shirt. Next to the driver was one of Dodi's bodyguards, an athletic, handsome Englishman and former army paratrooper named Trevor Rees-Jones, twenty-nine years old. An hour later, the Fayed's private jet, a Gulfstream IV, took off from the Olbia airport and headed for Paris. A tip-off to two freelance Sardinian journalists enabled them to get a few photos of the couple at the airport, and from there it was only minutes until the British tabloids were notified and swung into action.

When the plane landed at 3:20 that Saturday afternoon at Le Bourget, north of Paris, two dozen photographers were on hand. From inside the plane, Dodi sent a message demanding a police escort into town. "Diana was very calm," said one of the staff later, "but Dodi was annoyed and said they did not want to be followed, that they must avoid the cameras." They had, after all, only one night in Paris, and they wanted to leave the airport quickly. "We're in a hurry," Dodi told an airport representative of Louis Demarque's security staff. "We need to get away as soon as possible."

Within moments, a dark green Range Rover and a black Mercedes pulled onto the tarmac, both vehicles dispatched from the Ritz. One driver was the hotel's assistant director of security, who often met important guests. His name was Henri Paul, and he took the luggage in the Range Rover and proceeded to Dodi's Paris apartment to deposit it there; Dodi and Diana, meanwhile, went off in the Mercedes with Dodi's regular chauffeur, Philippe Dourneau. At about 3:50, they arrived at the post-war home of the Duke and Duchess of Windsor, purchased (as is the French custom) on a lease of one million francs a year by Mohamed al-Fayed in 1987. He completely refurbished and restored the mansion and was preparing to auction 40,000 items in its inventory. Diana had never visited the house before, and Dodi gave her a tour.

Then it was off to the Place Vendôme, where the driver bypassed the usual lineup of limousines. Security cameras at the Ritz recorded the arrival of Dodi and Diana in the black Mercedes at 4:35. At the same time, a small crew of photographers began to gather outside the hotel and at the rear entrance in the Rue Cambon. Greeted by senior staff, the couple were escorted to the Imperial Suite (fee: $10,000 per night, unless your father owns the hotel). The suite is aptly named, for its double bedroom, living and dining room, and baths are furnished with eighteenth-century antiques, chandeliers and oil paintings.

Dodi and Diana made a few telephone calls, he to a Malibu broker, who confirmed his purchase of a fabulous property once owned by Julie Andrews; she to journalist Richard Kay of London's *Daily Mail*, an old friend, confidant and conduit of her viewpoint to a waiting world. "All was well in her world," said Kay later. "She was as happy as I ever heard her." Diana told him she would fulfill her engagements through November and then retire—but this she had said at least twice before and then rescinded, pitching herself back into public life with renewed energy.

To Kay, she said nothing that indicated an imminent marriage; but Dodi, on a call to cousin Hassan Yassin, said he was about to marry Diana. Perhaps he took that as settled from the gifts they exchanged. Diana had given him a pair of her father's cuff links and a gold cigar clipper inscribed "With love from Diana," while (according to the Fayed family) Dodi had ordered a diamond ring costing $205,400 from the Paris jeweler Alberto Repossi. This gift was never found anywhere—neither in the wrecked car nor on Diana's finger. Meantime, a hairstylist was sent up for Diana, and a maid attended to her clothes.

Once again, the couple could not be detained anywhere for very long—it was as if they were suffused by a certain kind of hypertense, nervous energy. For people who ostensibly wished to avoid the media, they spent an inordinate amount of time going out. At precisely 7:15, they arrived in the black Mercedes at the Fayeds' Paris apartment used by Dodi, a second-floor residence at 1 Rue Arsène-Houssaye, at the corner of Champs-Elysées and a few steps from the Arc de Triomphe.

A table had been booked for two (in the name of the Ritz Hotel manager) at 8:45 at the renowned bistro Chez Benoît on Rue Saint-

Martin, near the Centre Pompidou. Because the hotel staff had been told Diana and Dodi would not return to the Ritz that night, Henri Paul confirmed Diana's flight to London for the next day and was then told his work that evening was complete. With that, he took his cellular phone and left the hotel.

At forty-one, Henri Paul was apparently a conscientious man, admired in his security work and liked by friends, clients and acquaintances. He frequently spent weekends in Lorient, his hometown in Brittany on the Atlantic; there, the barman at Le Be Bop Café recalled that Paul was not an excessive drinker, that he often preferred coffee, and never boasted of his position at the grandest hotel in the nation's capital. Also in Lorient, Paul's friend Jean-Jacques Guillou taught him to ride the powerful Honda VMAX motorbike. "He liked to pose with it," said Guillou, "but that was all. He was a good driver and a safe one, and he never drove it anywhere near its top speed, which was about 130 miles per hour. Also, he was a serious man and a friend to Dodi." Barmen in Paris had the same impression: Henri Paul was a moderate drinker—a glass or two of beer or wine was his limit.

For these reasons, and because he had passed advanced courses in driving techniques for luxury limousines and because he spoke fluent English and acceptable German, Henri Paul was trusted as an alternate driver at the Ritz, where his salary was about $40,000 a year. "He was known to be extremely competent," said a colleague. "If you gave him a job, he got it done without any problems." Claude Luc, a union representative for the Ritz employees, characterized Paul as "always very serious," but that was expected at the hotel. "If one of the Fayeds gives you an order, you follow it. No questions asked."

At 8:45, Diana and Dodi glanced out the windows of the apartment on Rue Arsène-Houssaye and saw a small platoon of paparazzi.

That meant a similar group would be gathering at Chez Benoît, so they canceled their reservation and instead decided to dine at the Ritz, where they would be politely ignored by everyone except the staff. At 9:30, they left the apartment and ducked into the Mercedes: Diana wore white slacks, a black jersey top and black jacket; Dodi sported Western boots, blue jeans, a gray shirt and a brown jacket.

At 9:50 (the Ritz security cameras documented the evening's activities there), the car arrived back at the Ritz. Now there were almost fifty photographers confronting a dozen security men outside the hotel. Mobile phones rang, messages were flashed round the world, photos were promised, deals made. Amid the general mayhem, Dodi and Diana sprinted into Espadon, the hotel's dining room. But a hush fell over the place and they became the center of everyone's attention—and so they decided, almost immediately, to abandon *this* location and instead to order dinner upstairs in seclusion, in the Imperial Suite.

But Dodi made it clear to the hotel staff that they would not be spending the night there: they would return to his apartment. Once again, such constant comings and goings were not exactly the way to discourage media attention—which was, it seems, like an aphrodisiac to Dodi al-Fayed. That Diana went along with him shows the extent to which she wanted to rely fully on this man. Alone, with friends or her sons, she would very likely have remained in one location that night in Paris.

Once alerted that the couple would eventually leave the hotel yet again to return to Rue Arsène-Houssaye, the night manager of the Ritz contacted Henri Paul on his portable telephone, asking him to return to the hotel and be prepared, in his capacity as assistant director of security, to chauffeur the couple later that evening.

Paul returned to the Place Vendôme, parked in the underground garage and entered the hotel, where he met Trevor Rees-Jones and other members of the Fayed retinue. No one at the Ritz noticed any inebriation as the team discussed the best way to shuttle their charges out of the Ritz and back to the flat with the least harassment. As it happened, Paul came up with the plan. He would collect Diana and Dodi at the back of the hotel, they would proceed south on the Rue Cambon and around the cobbled breadth of the Place de la Concorde to the Seine. Then Paul would drive west on the Cours la Reine and Cours Albert Premier, and, via the underpass at the Pont de l'Alma, north along Avenue Marceau toward the Arc de Triomphe and the Rue Arsène-Houssaye.

Such a scheme would, they hoped, either throw off any pursuing photographers or lead them to presume that such a route was taking the couple to the Windsor mansion. An additional ploy was set up: from 10:30, four more cars were arranged—including another black Mercedes and the green Range Rover—in plain sight in the Place Vendôme. There, the scenario included security personnel and doormen, telling the paparazzi they had only a few minutes to take pictures when Dodi and Diana emerged at eleven.

But when nothing happened by midnight, some of the reporters fanned out toward the Rue Cambon.

Shortly after midnight, the journey began.

At precisely 12:15 A.M. on Sunday, August 31, 1997, the security staff of the Ritz Hotel were alerted.

Dodi and Diana were ready to depart through the rear entrance of the hotel. The green Range Rover and the decoy black Mercedes (the latter driven by the hotel's senior limousine driver) pulled out into the Place Vendôme, circled the square and then returned to their parking spots. The photographers there were stymied.

Meantime, the second black 1994 Mercedes S-280, with Henri Paul at the wheel and Trevor Rees-Jones in the passenger seat, sped away from the rear of the Ritz; Dodi was behind Paul, Diana on his right, behind Rees-Jones. In the evident excitement, only Rees-Jones fastened his seat belt. It was 12:20 when the car sped south on Rue Cambon, then west along Rue de Rivoli and past the splashing, illuminated fountain and Egyptian obelisk of the Place de la Concorde. By the time the Mercedes was hugging the Seine and heading toward the underpass, the few paparazzi on motorbikes had dropped behind. Photographs of speeding cars (more to the point, of their occupants) are notoriously difficult to obtain at night; besides, the windows of the Mercedes were heavily tinted. Nor did any of these men wish to risk their lives by edging their bikes close to a speeding vehicle.

By the time Henri Paul and his passengers entered the Alma tunnel, the photographers were almost a quarter mile behind, keeping the car in sight but not endangering themselves by approaching the Mercedes. It would be enough to arrive at Dodi's apartment, where several colleagues of the pursuing paparazzi had already been alerted.

But another limousine driver entered the tunnel not far behind Paul, and this driver made a sworn statement of what happened— events that occurred within a few seconds, changing the course of countless lives and, it may be said without hyperbole, altering the course of late-twentieth-century history. The driver's account, it must be said, was in every way supported by police and by later forensic investigations of the site. And it is important to add that all police and official investigations discounted the proximity of paparazzi with blinding flashbulbs, on motorcycles.

Paul entered the tunnel on the left of two lanes and speeding at sixty to perhaps eighty or ninety miles an hour, which is not at all unusual in European cities—and then he found that his car was behind a slower vehicle. Careful though this driver might otherwise have been, it is easy to imagine Dodi urging him on: "Faster! Lose them! Go on!"—as, friends and colleagues recalled, he usually did. Life was a chase Dodi wanted to win, a game in which he wanted both to be in the limelight and to retain his privacy. Henri Paul, in a healthier condition, may well have been more cautious, but as Claude Luc said, Fayed employees did what they were told—period.

Paul veered the Mercedes to the right, to pass the car ahead of him in the left lane. But then everything went out of control, and the right rear of the Mercedes swerved and hit the right wall of the tunnel with a loud crash. Attempting to correct the situation, Paul turned sharply left—and within seconds the Mercedes crashed into one of the reinforced concrete dividing pillars that separated the lanes from oncoming traffic and also supported the roof. This time the sound, like an explosion, was nearly deafening.

The car ricocheted again, hurtling across the drive and spinning around before coming to a full stop. It had been immediately reduced to a barely recognizable mound of steel: the front end telescoped into the engine, which was forced almost through the driver's seat. Inside the pile of rubble, Henri Paul and Dodi al-Fayed were dead, their bodies hideously mangled. Trevor Rees-Jones was seriously injured, but Diana, Princess of Wales, was near death.

It was 12:24.

Approaching in his car from the opposite direction, Dr. Frédéric Mailliez stopped and ran to the spot. He saw at once that two of the passengers were dead, but that two others, including a blond woman, were perhaps still alive. Within seconds, the pursuing photographers had caught up. At the same time, police- and firemen arrived, alerted by cars exiting the tunnel ahead of the Mercedes; very soon, they identified the woman passenger.

By 1:15, the bodies of Henri Paul and Dodi al-Fayed had been removed from the wreck; later, after repeated toxicological tests, it was determined that Paul's blood contained four times the legal amount of alcohol permitted for drivers. There was also, in his system, evidence of two prescription medications for psychological and emotional stress: these were fluoxetine, which is the generic name for the American drug Prozac, and tiapride, a European compound often used to calm aggressive patients being treated for alcoholism.

Diana and Rees-Jones—both of them barely alive—took longer to extricate. Jean-Pierre Chevènement, the Interior Minister, was contacted by senior police officials and sped to the Hôpital de la Pitié-Salpêtrière, where Diana and Rees-Jones were taken. They arrived at 2:00 that morning.

A team of surgeons and nurses set to work on Rees-Jones, who underwent the first of many operations to reset and restructure his shattered jaw and broken arm. Subsequently, he was in a coma for weeks and had little memory of anything after the car left the hotel.

Diana's condition, however, was morbid.

A surgical team labored over her for almost two hours. She had sustained massive chest injuries and had bled profusely, and now a vein was severed and her blood pressure dropped to a dangerous level. At first it seemed that her age and fitness might grant some hope even in light of these traumas. But then it became clear that, despite the successful repair of the torn vein, all her internal organs were gravely damaged. She suffered cardiac arrest, and her heart failed to respond to open massage. Electric shocks were unavailing.

At 4:00 that morning, August 31, 1997, Diana, Princess of Wales, was pronounced dead.

10

THE LADY OF THE LAKE

Now folds the lily all her sweetness up,
And slips into the bosom of the lake.

—TENNYSON, *The Princess*

September 1997

Not long after the accident but before the details were clear, Interior Minister Jean-Pierre Chevènement telephoned Sir Michael Jay, the British ambassador to France. Jay then rang Robin Janvrin, assistant private secretary to the Queen, who was staying at Balmoral Castle with members of the Royal Family. Janvrin at once woke Prince Charles and told him that Diana had been seriously hurt, but that little else was known. At the same time, Mohamed al-Fayed received news of his son's injuries from the French—and then, by an odd trick of fate, Dodi's death was confirmed to him by none other than Diana's stepmother, Raine Spencer de Chambrun, who reached Fayed on his portable phone as he arrived at the hospital. She had heard the news on the BBC.

Charles decided, since the precise extent of Diana's injuries was still unclear, to awaken only his mother; he also called Camilla Parker

Bowles. But after conferring with two of his staff, Charles chose not to awaken his sons—even after news of Diana's death was confirmed at 3:00 British time (France is an hour ahead). Some time after seven that morning, when the boys awoke and were preparing to attend services at the local church with the Royal Family, Charles went to his sons with the awful news. One of the staff has acknowledged that Prince William said quietly, "I knew something was wrong. I kept waking up all night."

And then a curious set of instructions was issued, from no less a person than Her Majesty the Queen.

No newspapers were to be permitted at Balmoral until further notice; televisions and radios were not to be turned on; and Diana was not to be mentioned at all in royal precincts. The Queen further ordered that at the church services they were about to attend, the name of the Princess of Wales was not to be heard in prayers for the dead. Intending for the Royal Family to remain in Scotland until Diana's body was returned to England and a private funeral could be held, the Queen hoped that the entire event would pass, like an unfortunate cloud over the castle, and that soon life would resume its normal course. Tragedies do happen, but the realm and the Royal Family must go on forever. The tradition of the stiff upper lip so prevailed that it seemed amazing that anyone at Balmoral could actually speak about Diana's death.

The first poignant effect of this unreal (not to say callous) attitude was that William and Harry—doubtless dazed and not yet fully aware of the loss, which would of course need time to be absorbed—arrived at church with their father and, when Diana was not mentioned, turned to Charles and asked: "Are you sure Mummy is dead?"

Alas, for the moment the only official note of mourning was sounded by Prime Minister Tony Blair, who met the press at his home district in the village of Trimdon, County Durham.

"I feel like everyone else in this country today, utterly devastated.

"Our thoughts and prayers are with Princess Diana's family and in particular her two sons, the two boys.

"Our hearts go out to them. We are today a nation in Great Britain in a state of shock and in grief that is so deeply painful for us.

"She was a wonderful and warm human being, though her own life was often sadly touched by tragedy.

"She touched the lives of so many others in Britain and throughout the world with joy and comfort.

"How many times shall we remember her and in how many different ways? With the sick, the dying, with children, with the needy— when, with just a look or a gesture that spoke so much more than words, she would reveal to all of us the depth of her compassion and her humanity. You know how difficult things were for her from time to time. I'm sure we can only guess that, but the people everywhere, not just here in Britain, everywhere, kept faith with Princess Diana.

"They liked her. They loved her and regarded her as one of the people. She was the people's princess and that is how she will stay and how she will remain in our hearts and our memories forever.

"She seemed full of happiness and full of life. She was great fun to be with.

"She was unusual but a really warm character and personality. I will remember her personally with very great affection. I think the whole country will remember her with the very deepest affection and love. That is why our grief is so deep today."

Then things happened quickly. The boys were whisked back to Balmoral and placed in the care of their grandparents and the royal attendants, while Charles went to Aberdeen and on to Paris, where he was joined by Diana's sisters, Lady Jane Fellowes and Lady Sarah McCorquodale. There, the necessary painful legal details were dispatched, they met with the surgeons who had worked so long to save Diana, and they spoke briefly with Jacques Chirac, the President of France. Before the end of the day, Diana's coffin was returned to England with Charles and her sisters. Still, no decision had been made about the funeral or burial.

For five days, the British Royal Family retreated into its grief, giving the world (or at least the news media) an impression of emotionless, unsympathetic detachment. It would be difficult, indeed ridiculous, to imagine that the man Diana called "an excellent father" was unaffected and did not console his sons. But if any of Charles's family felt the sharp grief besieging the country, they gave no public sign of it; more to the point, the nation was anxious to see from its sovereign leader that the woman who had been the most beloved Windsor in living memory meant as much to them as she had to the British people and, indeed, the world. Never had the fundamental changes in social expression and expectation so confounded and confronted a monarchy that was still living in the distant past.

All during the week—while England and much of the world grieved and hundreds of thousands of mourners poured into London in an unprecedented rush of communal feeling—there was not a peep from the Queen, her court or her family. By Wednesday, the London newspapers were openly criticizing the royal indifference, and this was conveyed by Prime Minister Tony Blair to Prince Charles. Still, the family remained secluded at Balmoral, emotionally isolated and out of step with the people they were consecrated to serve, encourage and comfort. Friends and relatives of royal cousins called the castle, too—all to no avail. Since Diana's death, two brief messages had left from Balmoral, and neither of them mentioned Diana.

Finally, Geoffrey Crawford, the Queen's senior press secretary, was commanded to make a statement. "The Royal Family have been hurt," he said, presenting the clan as a grieving, defensive brood of mourners, "by suggestions that they are indifferent to the country's sorrow at the tragic death of the Princess of Wales. The Princess was a much loved national figure, but she was also a mother whose sons miss her deeply."

There was then an attempt to manipulate the disappointed public by turning attention to the grieving boys. "Prince William and Prince Harry themselves want to be with their father and grandparents at this time in the quiet haven of Balmoral. As their grandmother, the Queen is helping the Princes to come to terms with their loss."

Finally, Charles had enough. Weeks later, London newspapers reported that, at the age of forty-eight and for perhaps the first time in his life, the Prince of Wales stood up to his mother. Threatening that if she did not say something to the nation, if she did not move the court to London and involve them all in the rituals of mourning, he would forthwith take his sons and proceed on his own.

According to friends who had known him since childhood, Charles saw clearly that the love and respect Diana enjoyed in life must be honored in death. She represented a new kind of British attitude—such was the message Tony Blair was stressing in his conversations with Charles—an attitude that surmounted the classical divisions of caste, race, wealth, stamina and gender orientation. Although Diana was no revolutionary, she was a woman of her time and she included all the marginalized in the circle of her life. The poor were her compatriots, the anxious were her brothers and sisters, the ill were her concern, artists, designers and rock stars were in her social circle, homosexuals were among her friends, and she took a Muslim for her lover.

Charles's confrontation with his mother had the predictable effect: it was announced that the Queen, Prince Philip, Prince Charles and Princes William and Harry would arrive in London on Thursday, that Her Majesty would address the nation on television Friday afternoon, and that a funeral service would be held at Westminster Abbey on Saturday morning. The Prime Minister had insisted that the funeral be held then, so that working people would be free either to line the streets of London or to watch the services on television.

On Friday, September 5, 1997, Her Majesty Queen Elizabeth II addressed the nation and the world; this was only the second time in her forty-five-year reign that she had spoken to her subjects, outside of the traditional Christmas greeting (the first had been during the Gulf War). In measured words and in a controlled manner that witnessed a lifetime of doing things as impersonally as possible and as affectlessly as she believed her station required, the Queen faced the camera and declaimed in her usual flat tone:

"Since last Sunday's dreadful news, we have seen, throughout Britain and around the world, an overwhelming expression of sadness at Diana's death. We have all been trying in our different ways to cope.

"It is not easy to express a sense of loss, since the initial shock is often succeeded by a mixture of other feelings: disbelief, incomprehension, anger and concern for those who remain.

"We have all felt those emotions in these last few days. So what I say to you now, as your Queen and as a grandmother, I say from my heart.

"First, I want to pay tribute to Diana myself. She was an exceptional and gifted human being. In good times and bad, she never lost her capacity to smile and laugh, nor to inspire others with her warmth and kindness.

"I admired and respected her for her energy and commitment to others, and especially for her devotion to her two boys.

"This week at Balmoral we have all been trying to help William and Harry come to terms with the devastating loss that they and the rest of us have suffered.

"No one who knew Diana will ever forget her. Millions of others who never met her, but felt they knew her, will remember her. I, for one, believe that there are lessons to be drawn from her life and from the extraordinary and moving reaction to her death.

"I share in your determination to cherish her memory.

"This is also an opportunity for me, on behalf of my family, and especially Prince Charles and William and Harry, to thank all of you who have brought flowers, sent messages and paid your respects in so many ways to a remarkable person. These acts of kindness have been a huge source of help and comfort.

"Our thoughts are also with Diana's family and the families of those who died with her.

"I know that they, too, have drawn strength from what has happened since last weekend, as they seek to heal their sorrow and then to face the future without a loved one.

"I hope that tomorrow we can all, wherever we are, join in expressing our grief at Diana's loss, and gratitude for her all too short life.

"It is a chance to show to the whole world the British nation united in grief and respect. May those who died rest in peace and may we, each and every one of us, thank God for someone who made many, many people happy."

Some people were moved by the Queen's statement (if not made happy), but the appearance in public of Diana's sons, William and

Harry, surveying the flowers at Balmoral, was a balm. When the boys arrived in London on Friday, they gamely went to meet the crowds outside Kensington Palace. More than a million bouquets had been placed there by this time, and when the boys shyly shook the hands of many in the crowd and thanked them for their condolences, the events suddenly took on the vague tint of a runoff in a parliamentary election. Only the bemused looks on the boys' faces revealed that they might not have comprehended the curious mixture of sadness and thrill that their presence caused the masses. More than once, Harry reached for his father's hand; William smiled, as he had been taught to do since early years. It was touching and somehow also unreal.

Around the world, it was estimated that almost three billion people watched the ceremony on Saturday, each of them drawn to a common ritual of grief for a woman few of them knew. Diana, Princess of Wales, was dead, and her funeral rites were duly and impressively performed. Although at her death she was no longer a member of England's premiere family, the outside world seems to have considered her the most royal of all people. There was about her a refreshing sense of ordinariness. From the first day, she was often referred to affectionately as "Lady Di." This friendly informality, too, was unprecedented. Can you imagine any other member of the Royal Family evoking a nickname? Would anyone be tempted to refer to the queen as "Liz" or "Betty," to suggest that Princess Margaret be called "Peggy"? Does Prince Charles inspire the nickname "Charlie" or "Chuck"? She was an aristocrat by birth but she was different from the royals: accessible, warm and a true citizen of her time, she *was* the people's Princess.

The general lamentation for the lost Diana had no parallel in our time. For comparison, one would have to cast the net of memory back to the sudden deaths of John Kennedy and of his brother Robert, of

Martin Luther King, and of pop stars like Rudolph Valentino, James Dean, Marilyn Monroe, Elvis Presley and John Lennon. But even the international attention given to these events paled in comparison with that of Diana's death.

As we all have seen before, her sudden passing will freeze her in time, so that she will never grow old in the public consciousness, never lose her appeal or her popularity, never become stale news or forfeit the exciting part she chose to play on the world's stage. In this regard, Diana was not merely the representative of a certain time or country, and her allure went beyond the boundaries of nation or class. And she was indeed of the past when she married the heir to the world's most prestigious throne. But her temperament was modern and everything shifted as she became an active, articulate Windsor with many dedicated causes to trumpet. When her marriage went sour, remarkably, instead of withdrawing into selfish isolation, she identified with the world's suffering even more. Every day she tried to make a difference. In the last year of her life, she was emerging like a butterfly from a chrysalis. Who is to say what this extraordinary woman might have accomplished with more time, for time was all she lacked.

The absolute correctness, the telling simplicity and solemnity that characterized the memorial service at Westminster Abbey were sublime in every aspect—there were music and poetry from the past and present, all of it comprising a reverent ritual for a needy world grown dissatisfied with empty formalism.

At her marriage in 1981, all people could indulge their fantasies—the event was actually called, by none other than the Archbishop of Canterbury, "the stuff of fairy tales." But fairy tales rarely coincide with reality.

Nevertheless, sixteen years before her death the fable was promulgated. A shy, lovely virgin, plucked from obscurity, wed the handsome Prince who needed a consort to secure the monarchy. The story had every archetype of an upper-class *Cinderella:* an intrusive step-mother, two older sisters regarded as prettier rivals, an adoration of small animals. There was even a fairy godmother to plan the marriage—in this case, the Queen Mother, whose closest friend and lady-in-waiting happened to be Diana's grandmother, Ruth, Lady Fermoy. Together, the two ladies hatched the scheme.

The deal was struck, and Diana married the Prince. This turned out to be an impossible dream for her and everyone else, although it took a while before we learned the awful truth: that Charles had a true love elsewhere. To paraphrase Cromwell: this was not France (where such circumstances are traditionally taken for granted), this was England, and so the poor girl was devastated, the dream immediately ended and the nightmare began.

Not all of us marry, few are rich, and still fewer are famous or glamorous. But we all die, and Diana's death once again revealed with disturbing immediacy that even the most beautiful among us, the young, the affluent, the desirable, the charming—those who seem to have it all as well as the freedom to indulge every whim for luxury and to explore every impulse—can be snatched from life in the twinkling of an eye. Rightly did the Dean of Westminster conclude the funeral with an offering to God of our own mortality and vulnerability.

In the year since her divorce, Diana was drawn to the heady rush of a freewheeling romantic life. That she had so recently selected a Muslim playboy for the object of her affections is not as surprising as it seems, for in this way she added revenge to the romance: Dodi al-Fayed's father had been denied British citizenship despite the fact that he owned Harrods, Britain's fanciest department store. Diana's *aventure* and perhaps her subsequent marriage to a man of color would have outraged class-conscious Buckingham Palace even more than her maverick charitable causes and her earlier love affairs. But for Diana, skewering convention was itself a kind of retribution, and it may have played a significant part in the mind of this honest and honorable but complex woman.

Shortly after she married, she answered a letter from her nursery schoolgirls, those who had known her as their teacher "Miss Diana" a year earlier. "I hope to see you all again one day," she replied. "Until then, be good." And although she was now a royal personage, she did not sign the letter "Diana P"—for "Princess," as protocol required. Instead, she signed plainly, "Love from Miss Diana."

That directness and simplicity, that lack of pomposity and easy connection with children and with all ranks of people, were perfectly captured in the eulogy offered by her brother, Charles Spencer, at the funeral at Westminster Abbey on September 6, 1997.

"I stand before you today the representative of a family in grief, in a country in mourning, before a world in shock.

"We are all united not only in our desire to pay our respects to Diana, but rather in our need to do so.

"For such was her extraordinary appeal that the tens of millions of people taking part in this service all over the world via television and radio who never actually met her, feel that they too lost someone close to them in the early hours of Sunday morning. It is a more remarkable tribute to Diana than I can ever hope to offer her today.

"Diana was the very essence of compassion, of duty, of style, of beauty. All over the world she was a symbol of selfless humanity. All over the world, a standard bearer for the rights of the truly down-trodden, a very British girl who transcended nationality—someone with a natural nobility who was classless and who proved in the last year that she needed no royal title to continue to generate her partic-ular brand of magic.

"Today is our chance to say thank you for the way you brightened our lives, even though God granted you but half a life. We will all feel cheated always that you were taken from us so young, and yet we must learn to be grateful that you came along at all. Only now that you are gone do we truly appreciate what we are now without and we want you to know that life without you is very, very difficult.

"We have all despaired at our loss over the past week and only the strength of the message you gave us through your years of giving has afforded us the strength to move forward.

"There is a temptation to rush to canonize your memory, but there is no need to do so. You stand tall enough as a human being of unique qualities not to need to be seen as a saint. Indeed, to sanctify your memory would be to miss out on the very core of your being, your wonderful mischievous sense of humor with a laugh that bent you double.

"Your joy for life transmitted wherever you took your smile and the sparkle in those unforgettable eyes. Your boundless energy which you could barely contain.

"But your greatest gift was your intuition and it was a gift you used wisely. This is what underpinned all your other wonderful attributes and if we look to analyze what it was about you that had such a wide appeal we find it in your instinctive feel for what was really important in all our lives. Without your God-given sensitivity we would be immersed in greater ignorance at the anguish of AIDS and HIV sufferers, the plight of the homeless, the isolation of lepers, the random destruction of land mines.

"Diana explained to me once that it was her innermost feelings of suffering that made it possible for her to connect with her constituency of the rejected. And here we come to another truth about her. For all the status, the glamour, the applause, Diana remained throughout a very insecure person at heart, almost childlike in her desire to do good for others so she could release herself from deep feelings of unworthiness of which her eating disorders were merely a symptom.

"The world sensed this part of her character and cherished her for her vulnerability while admiring her for her honesty.

"The last time I saw Diana was on July first, her birthday in London, when typically she was not taking time to celebrate her special day with friends but was guest of honor at a special charity fundraising evening. She sparkled of course, but I would rather cherish the days I spent with her in March when she came to visit me and my children in our home in South Africa. I am proud of the fact, apart from when she was on display meeting President Mandela, that we managed to contrive to stop the ever-present paparazzi from getting a single picture of her—that meant a lot to her.

"These were days I will always treasure. It was as if we had been transported back to our childhood when we spent such an enormous amount of time together—the two youngest in the family. Fundamentally she had not changed at all from the big sister who mothered me as a baby, fought with me at school and endured those long train journeys between our parents' homes with me at weekends.

"It is a tribute to her levelheadedness and strength that, despite the most bizarre life imaginable after her childhood, she remained intact, true to herself.

"There is no doubt that she was looking for a new direction in her life at this time. She talked endlessly of getting away from England, mainly because of the treatment that she received at the hands of the newspapers. I don't think she ever understood why her genuinely good intentions were sneered at by the media, why there appeared to be a permanent quest on their behalf to bring her down. It is baffling. My own and only explanation is that genuine goodness is threatening to those at the opposite end of the moral spectrum. It is a point to remember that of all the ironies about Diana, perhaps the greatest was this—a girl given the name of the ancient goddess of hunting was, in the end, the most hunted person of the modern age.

"She would want us today to pledge ourselves to protecting her beloved boys, William and Harry, from a similar fate—and I do this here, Diana, on your behalf. We will not allow them to suffer the anguish that used regularly to drive you to tearful despair.

"And beyond that, on behalf of your mother and sisters, I pledge that we, your blood family, will do all we can to continue the imaginative way in which you were steering these two exceptional young men so that their souls are not simply immersed by duty and tradition but can sing openly as you planned.

"We fully respect the heritage into which they have both been born and will always respect and encourage them in their royal role. But we, like you, recognize the need for them to experience as many different aspects of life as possible—to arm them spiritually and emotionally for the years ahead. I know you would have expected nothing less from us.

"William and Harry, we all care desperately for you today. We are all chewed up with the sadness at the loss of a woman who was not even our mother. How great your suffering is, we cannot even imagine.

"I would like to end by thanking God for the small mercies He has shown us at this dreadful time—for taking Diana at her most beautiful and radiant and when she had joy in her private life. Above all we give thanks for the life of a woman I am so proud to be able to call my sister, the unique, the complex, the extraordinary and irreplaceable Diana whose beauty, both internal and external, will never be extinguished from our minds."

At the conclusion of the funeral service, the coffin was put into a closed hearse, which began its two-hour journey to Althorp House, Diana's ancestral home, seventy-five miles northwest of London. Slowly the car made its way, and, along the route, it was many times covered with bouquets, tossed as a last, loving gesture. Bystanders applauded; many wiped tears from their eyes; all the people, it seemed, were waving their Princess into eternity.

The cortege was the only northbound traffic on the motorway, and en route southbound vehicles stopped as it passed. Drivers and passengers climbed out and stood in reverence.

By late afternoon, Diana's mother, sisters and brother were on the vast and green land of the Spencer clan. Soon they were joined by Prince Charles, Prince William and Prince Harry—all of them red-eyed, flushed and weary.

Earl Spencer had elected, at first, to bury his sister in the thirteenth-century church of St. Mary in nearby Great Brington, where the Spencer family crypt contains twenty generations. But then he decided that Diana's final resting place should be more private, less accessible to pilgrims and to possible vandalism, and so he settled on burying her on a small green island in the center of a lake at Althorp—an island called The Oval, which had been a favorite spot for them as teens on holiday. Here they had played on summer days; here they sat, watching the geese fly and the sheep wander nearby, chasing fireflies in the long twilights, spinning dreams and plans for their futures. The island was a space of great security to the children, its tiny, sixty-by-twenty-five-yard parcel of land as infinite as the universe.

At last there were no photographers, no flashbulbs, no jostling for position. The public was not allowed onto the grounds for the burial, and the airspace above was forbidden to all planes for the rest of the day and into the evening.

The family gathered quietly, and as the sky clouded there was for a moment some fear of rain. But then the sun, low on the horizon by midevening, shone through brilliantly. On the island, a simple grave facing east had been prepared, shaded by willow, oak and beech trees. There was a brief ceremony, and then all withdrew. Just before darkness, there was a gentle rain, and when that passed, the starlings began to sing, as if there were no night at all.

Bibliography

Allison, Ronald, and Sarah Riddell, eds. *The Royal Encyclopedia.* London: Macmillan, 1991.

Alsop, Susan Mary. *To Marietta from Paris.* New York: Doubleday, 1975.

————. "The Monarchy Today," *The National & English Review,* Aug. 1957.

Amory, Cleveland. *The Best Cat Ever.* Boston: Little, Brown, 1993.

————. *Who Killed Society?* New York: Harper & Bros., 1960.

Arnold, Harry. "How Those Gay Rumors Started," *Daily Mirror,* Apr. 10, 1990.

Arnstein, Walter L. "Queen Victoria Opens Parliament: The Disinvention of Tradition," *Historical Research,* June 1990.

Aronson, Theo. *Royal Family: Years of Transition.* London: John Murray, 1983.

————. *The Royal Family At War.* London: John Murray, 1993.

Asquith, Lady Cynthia. *The King's Daughters.* London: Hutchinson, 1937.

Atkinson, A. B. *Unequal Shares.* Harmondsworth: Penguin, 1974.

Austin, Victoria. "Charles, Diana and the Dilemmas of Divorce," *Royalty,* autumn 1993.

Bagehot, Walter. *The English Constitution.* London: Kegan Paul, 1898; alternately, Oxford: The University Press, 1929 edition.

Bailey, Gilbert. "She Could Charm the Pearl Out of an Oyster," *The New York Times Magazine,* Aug. 21, 1949.

BIBLIOGRAPHY

Barker, Malcolm J., with T. C. Sobey. *Living With the Queen.* Fort Lee, N.J.: Barricade Books, 1991.

Barry, Stephen. *Royal Service.* New York: Avon, 1983.

Battine, Cecil. "Our Monarchy and Its Alliances," *The Fortnightly Review,* Sept. 1917.

Battiscombe, Georgina. *Queen Alexandra.* London: Constable, 1969.

Baxter, A. B. *Destiny Called to Them.* Oxford: The University Press, 1939.

Beard, Madeleine. *English Landed Society in the 20th Century.* London: Routledge, 1989.

Bedfordshire Times and Independent. Aug. 1921.

Benson, E. F. *Queen Victoria.* London: Longmans, Green, 1935.

Bentley-Cranch, Dana. *Edward VII.* London: HMSO, 1992.

Birkenhead, Lord. *Walter Monckton.* London: Hamish Hamilton, 1969.

Boothroyd, Basil. *Philip, An Informal Biography.* London: Longman, 1971.

Botham, Noel. *Margaret: The Untold Story.* London: Blake, 1994.

Bradford, Sarah. *The Reluctant King: The Life & Reign of George VI, 1895–1952.* New York: St. Martin's, 1989.

British Medical Journal, May 1910.

Broad, Lewis. *The Abdication: Twenty-five Years After.* London: Frederick Muller, 1961.

Bryan, J., III, and Charles J. V. Murphy. *The Windsor Story.* New York: William Morrow, 1979.

Buckle, G. E., ed. *The Letters of Queen Victoria: A Selection from Her Majesty's Correspondence Between the Years 1862 and 1885.* London: John Murray, 1926.

Campbell, Lady Colin. *Diana in Private*. London: Smith Gryphon, 1993.

Cannadine, David. *The Decline and Fall of the British Aristocracy*. New Haven: Yale University Press, 1990.

Cannon, John, and Ralph Griffiths. *The Oxford Illustrated History of the British Monarchy*. Oxford and New York: Oxford University Press, 1992.

Carey, M. C. *Princess Mary*. London: Nisbet, 1922.

Cathcart, Helen. *The Queen Herself.* London: W. H. Allen, 1983.

———. *The Queen Mother*. London: W. H. Allen, 1965.

———. *The Queen and Prince Philip: Forty Years of Happiness*. London: Coronet/Hodder and Stoughton, 1987.

———. *The Royal Bedside Book*. London: W. H. Allen, 1969.

Chase, Edna Woolman, and Ilka Chase. *Always in Vogue*. London: Victor Gollancz, 1954.

Christopher, Prince of Greece. *Memoirs of HRH Prince Christopher of Greece*. London: Hurst and Blackett, 1938.

Clark, Stanley. *Palace Diary*. London: Harrap, 1958.

Clarke, Mary. *Diana Once Upon a Time*. London: Sidgwick & Jackson, 1994.

Colville, John. *The Fringes of Power: Downing Street Diaries,* vol. 2, 1941–April 1955. London: Hodder and Stoughton, 1985.

Corby, Tom. *H. M. Queen Elizabeth the Queen Mother*. London: Award Publications, 1990.

Coughlan, Robert. "Britain's National Deb," *Life,* Oct. 31, 1949.

Crawford, Marion. *The Little Princesses*. London: Cassell, 1950.

———. *Queen Elizabeth II*. London: George Newnes, 1952.

BIBLIOGRAPHY

Critchfield, Richard. *An American Looks At Britain*. New York: Doubleday, 1990.

Davenport-Hines, Richard. "Margaret," *Tatler,* June 1992.

Davies, Nicholas. *Diana: A Princess and Her Troubled Marriage*. New York: Carol/Birch Lane, 1992.

————. *Diana: The Lonely Princess*. New York: Birch Lane/Carol, 1996.

De-la-Noy, Michael. *The Queen Behind the Throne*. London: Hutchinson, 1994.

Delderfield, Eric R. *Kings and Queens of England and Great Britain*. Newton Abbot and London: David & Charles, 1990.

Dell, John. "Prince Philip," *Cosmopolitan,* Mar. 1953.

Dempster, Nigel, and Peter Evans. *Behind Palace Doors*. New York: Putnam, 1993.

————. *HRH The Princess Margaret: A Life Unfulfilled*. London: Quartet, 1981.

Dimbleby, Jonathan. *The Prince of Wales: A Biography*. London: Little, Brown, 1994.

Dimbleby, Richard. *Elizabeth Our Queen*. London: University of London Press, 1953.

Donaldson, Frances. *Edward VIII*. London: Weidenfeld and Nicolson, 1974.

————. *King George VI and Queen Elizabeth*. London: Weidenfeld and Nicolson, 1977.

Dullea, Georgia. "Mercy, Mischief and a Royal Fiction," *The New York Times,* Feb. 16, 1994.

Duncan, Andrew. *The Reality of Monarchy*. London: Heinemann, 1970.

Edgar, Donald. *The Queen's Children.* Middlesex: Hamlyn Paperbacks, 1979.

Edwards, Anne. *Royal Sisters.* New York: Jove, 1991.

Elliott, Caroline, ed. *The BBC Book of Royal Memories.* Jersey City: Parkwest, 1994.

Ellis, Jennifer, ed. *Mabell Countess of Airlie, Thatched with Gold.* London: Hutchinson, 1962.

Ellison, John. "Wallis Windsor, Duchess in Exile," *Daily Express,* Feb. 13, 1979.

Erlich, Henry. "Anne of the Twenty Years," *Look,* July 28, 1970.

Fairley, Josephine. *Crown Princess: A Biography of Diana.* New York: St. Martin's Press, 1992.

————. *The Princess and the Duchess.* New York: St. Martin's, 1989.

Ferguson, Ronald. *The Galloping Major: My Life and Singular Times.* London: Macmillan, 1994.

Fisher, Baron J. A. F. *Memories.* London: Hodder & Stoughton, 1919.

Fisher, Clive. *Noël Coward.* London: Weidenfeld and Nicolson, 1992.

Fisher, Graham and Heather. "Princess Anne: Britain's Royal Swinger," *Good Housekeeping,* July 1970.

Flanner, Janet. *An American in Paris.* New York: Simon & Schuster, 1940.

————. *London Was Yesterday, 1934–1939.* London: Michael Joseph, 1975.

Fox, Mary Virginia. *Princess Diana.* Hillside, N.J.: Enslow, 1986.

Frankland, Noble. *Prince Henry, Duke of Gloucester.* London: Weidenfeld and Nicolson, 1980.

Friedman, Dennis. *Inheritance.* London: Sidgwick & Jackson, 1993.

BIBLIOGRAPHY

Frischauer, Willi. *Margaret: Princess Without a Cause*. London: Michael Joseph, 1977.

Fry, Plantagenet Somerset. *The Kings and Queens of England and Scotland*. New York: Grove Weidenfeld, 1990.

Giles, Frank. *Sundry Times*. London: John Murray, 1986.

Golby, J. W., and A. W. Purdue. *The Monarchy and the British People*. London: B. T. Batsford, 1988.

Gore, John. *King George the Fifth: A Personal Memoir*. London: John Murray, 1941.

Graham, Caroline. *Camilla—the King's Mistress: A Love Story*. London: Blake, 1994.

Graham, Tim. *Diana: HRH The Princess of Wales*. New York: Summit, 1988.

————. *The Royal Year 1991*. New York: Summit, 1991.

————. *The Royal Year 1992*. New York: Simon & Schuster, 1992.

————. *The Royal Year 1993*. London: Michael O'Mara, 1993.

Green, Michelle. "Royal Watch," *People,* Aug. 22, 1994.

Green, Michelle, and Terry Smith. "Diss and Tell," *People,* Oct. 17, 1994.

Greenslade, Roy. "Elizabeth the Last?—Down the Royals! Up the Republic!" *The Guardian,* Mar. 28, 1994.

Grigg, John. "Queen Elizabeth II," *The Listener,* Dec. 24, 1970.

Hall, Phillip. *Royal Fortune: Tax, Money and the Monarchy*. London: Bloomsbury, 1992.

Hall, Unity. *The Private Lives of Britain's Royal Women: Their Passions and Power*. Chicago: Contemporary Books, 1991.

Hall, Unity, and Ingrid Seward. *Royalty Revealed*. New York: St. Martin's Press, 1989.

Hamilton, Ronald. *Now I Remember*. London: Hogarth, 1984.

Harewood (Earl of), George (Lascelles). *The Tongs and the Bones*. London: Weidenfeld and Nicolson, 1981.

Heald, Tim. *Philip: A Portrait of the Duke of Edinburgh*. New York: William Morrow, 1991.

Hibbert, Christopher. *Edward VIII—A Portrait*. London: Penguin, 1982.

Hindley, Geoffrey. *The Guinness Book of British Royalty*. London: Guinness, 1989.

Hoey, Brian. *All the King's Men*. London: HarperCollins, 1992.

———. *Monarchy: Behind the Scenes with the Royal Family*. London: BBC Books, 1987.

———. *The New Royal Court*. Oxford: Isis, 1992.

Holden, Anthony. *Charles*. London: Weidenfeld and Nicolson, 1988.

———. *A Princely Marriage*. London: Bantam, 1991.

———. *The Tarnished Crown*. New York: Random House, 1993.

———. *Their Royal Highnesses*. London: Weidenfeld and Nicolson, 1981.

Holland, Henrietta. "The Royal Collection," *The Tatler*, Mar. 1994.

Hough, Richard. *Born Royal: The Lives and Loves of the Young Windsors*. New York: Bantam, 1988.

———. *Edward and Alexandra: Their Private and Public Lives*. London: John Curtis/Hodder and Stoughton, 1992.

Hull, Fiona Macdonald. "Diana's Battle Royal," *Ladies' Home Journal*, Apr. 1994.

BIBLIOGRAPHY

Hutchins, Chris, and Peter Thompson. *Sarah's Story: The Duchess Who Defied the Royal House of Windsor*. London: Smith Gryphon, 1992.

Inglis, Brian. *Abdication*. London: Hodder & Stoughton, 1966.

James, Paul. *Margaret: A Woman of Conflict*. London: Sidgwick and Jackson, 1990.

————. *Princess Alexandra*. London: Weidenfeld and Nicolson, 1992.

James, Robert Rhodes, ed. *Chips: The Diaries of Sir Henry Channon*. London: Weidenfeld and Nicolson, 1967.

Jay, Antony. *Elizabeth R*. London: BBC Books, 1992.

Jones, Thomas. *Whitehall Diary*, 2 vols. Oxford: The University Press, 1969 and 1971.

Judd, Denis. *The House of Windsor*. London: Macdonald, 1973.

————. *The Life and Times of George V*. London: Weidenfeld and Nicolson, 1993.

————. *Prince Philip*. London: Sphere, 1991.

Jullian, Philippe. *Edward and the Edwardians*. London: Sidgwick & Jackson, 1967.

Kay, Richard. "Anne Wanted Her Freedom," *Daily Mail*, Sept. 1, 1989.

————. "Revealed: secret heroism of Prince Philip's mother," *Daily Mail*, July 26, 1993.

Keay, Douglas. *Royal Pursuit: The Palace, The Press and The People*. London: Severn House Books, 1983.

Kenyon, J. P., ed. *Dictionary of British History*. Ware, England: Wordsworth Editions, 1992.

King, Stella. *Princess Marina, Her Life and Times*. London: Cassell, 1969.

Lacey, Robert. "The King and Mrs. Simpson," *Radio Times,* Dec. 3–10, 1976.

————. *Majesty.* 1977.

————. *Princess.* Toronto: McClelland and Stewart, 1982.

————. *Queen Mother.* Boston: Little, Brown, 1986.

Laguerre, Andre. "Clues to a Princess's Choice," *Life,* Oct. 10, 1955.

Lancet, The, Feb. 18, 1911.

Latham, Caroline, and Jeannie Sakol. *The Royals.* New York: Congdon & Weed, 1987.

Lee, Sydney. *King Edward VII,* 2 vols. London: Macmillan, 1927.

————. *Queen Victoria.* London: John Murray, 1904.

Lees-Milne, James. *The Enigmatic Edwardian: Life of Reginald Brett, Viscount Esher.* London: Sidgwick & Jackson, 1986.

————. *Harold Nicolson.* London: Chatto & Windus, 1981.

Levy, Alan. "Queen Elizabeth and Philip," *Good Housekeeping,* Nov. 1957.

Lewis, Brenda Ralph. "Queen Consort of England," *Royalty,* vol. 12 no. 8 (1993).

Licata, Renora. *Princess Diana: Royal Ambassador.* Woodbridge, Ct.: Blackbirch Press, 1993.

Litvinoff, Sarah, and Marianne Sinclair, eds. *The Wit and Wisdom of the Royal Family.* London: Plexus, 1990.

Lloyd George, David. *War Memoirs,* 6 vols. London: Nicholson and Watson, 1933–1936.

Lockhart, J. G. *Cosmo Gordon Lang.* London: Hodder & Stoughton, 1949.

Longford, Elizabeth. *Louisa, Lady-in-Waiting.* London: Roxby & Lindsey, 1979.

———. *The Oxford Book of Royal Anecdotes.* Oxford: The University Press, 1991.

———. *The Queen Mother.* London: Weidenfeld and Nicolson, 1981.

———. *The Royal House of Windsor.* London: Book Club Associates, 1974.

———. *Royal Throne.* London: John Curtis/Hodder & Stoughton, 1993.

———. *Victoria, R. I.* London: Weidenfeld and Nicolson, 1964.

Lovell, Mary. *Straight On Till Morning: The Life of Beryl Markham.* London: Century Hutchinson, 1987.

Lowry, Suzanne. *The Cult of Diana: The Princess in the Mirror.* Oxford: Isis, 1987.

Maclean, Veronica. *Crowned Heads.* London: Hodder & Stoughton, 1993.

Magnus, Philip. *Edward the Seventh.* London: John Murray, 1964.

Manchester, William. *The Last Lion.* Boston: Little, Brown, 1983.

Marie Louise, Princess. *My Memories of Six Reigns.* London: Evans, 1956.

Martin, Kingsley. "The Evolution of Popular Monarchy," *The Political Quarterly,* Apr. 1936.

———. "Strange Interlude: Edward VIII's Brief Reign," *The Atlantic,* May 1962.

Martin, Ralph G. *Charles & Diana.* New York: Putnam's, 1985.

Martin, Theodore. *Queen Victoria as I Knew Her.* Edinburgh, 1908.

Menkes, Suzy. *The Windsor Style.* London: Grafton, 1987.

Mercer, Derek, ed. *Chronicle of the Royal Family.* London: Chronicle Communications, 1991.

Metcalfe, James. *All the Queen's Children.* London: Star/W. H. Allen, 1981.

Middlemas, Keith. *The Life and Times of George VI.* London: Weidenfeld and Nicolson, 1974.

Middlemas, Keith, and John Barnes. *Baldwin.* London: Weidenfeld and Nicolson, 1969.

Montgomery-Massingberd, Hugh. *Burke's Guide to the British Monarchy.* London: Burke's Peerage, 1977.

————. *Debrett's Great British Families.* Exeter: Webb & Bower, 1988.

Monypenny, W. F., and G. E. Buckle, eds. *The Life of Benjamin Disraeli, Earl of Beaconsfield,* 6 vols. London: 1910–1920.

Moore, Sally. *The Definitive Diana.* Chicago: Contemporary Books, 1991.

Morley, Sheridan. *Gertrude Lawrence.* London: Weidenfeld and Nicolson, 1981.

Morrah, Dermot. *Princess Elizabeth.* London: Odhams, 1947.

Morrow, Ann. *Princess.* London: Chapman, 1991.

————. *The Queen.* Suffolk: Book Club Associates/Granada, 1983.

Morton, Andrew. *Diana: Her New Life.* London: Michael O'Mara, 1994.

————. *Diana: Her True Story.* London: Michael O'Mara, 1992.

————. *Inside Buckingham Palace.* London: Michael O'Mara, 1991.

————. *Theirs Is the Kingdom.* London: Michael O'Mara, 1989.

Moye, Hedda. "Hair: By Royal Appointment," *OK!,* May 1994.

BIBLIOGRAPHY

Munro-Wilson, Broderick. "In Praise of Camilla," *Daily Mail,* Nov. 24, 1994.

Murray-Brown, Jeremy, ed. *The Monarchy and Its Future.* London: Allen and Unwin, 1969.

Nairn, Tom. *The Enchanted Glass.* London: Picador, 1990. *New Idea,* Jan. 22, 1993.

Nicolson, Harold. *King George the Fifth.* London: Constable, 1952 (reprint: Pan, 1967).

Nicolson, Nigel, ed. *Harold Nicolson, Diaries and Letters.* London: Collins, 1968.

Parker, Eileen. *Step Aside For Royalty.* Maidstone, England: Bachman and Turner, 1982.

Parker, John. *Prince Philip.* London: Sidgwick & Jackson, 1990.

————. *The Princess Royal.* London: Coronet/Hodder and Stoughton, 1989.

————. *The Queen.* London: Headline, 1992.

Pasternak, Anna. *Princess in Love.* London: Bloomsbury, 1994.

Payn, Graham, and Sheridan Morley, eds. *The Noël Coward Diaries.* Boston: Little, Brown, 1983.

Pearson, John. *The Ultimate Family.* London: Michael Joseph, 1986.

Petrie, Sir Charles. *The Modern British Monarchy.* London: Eyre and Spottiswode, 1961.

Player, Leslie, with William Hall. *My Story: the Duchess of York, Her Father and Me.* London: Grafton/HarperCollins, 1993.

Ponsonby, Arthur. *Henry Ponsonby: His Life from His Letters.* London: Macmillan, 1942.

Ponsonby, Frederick. *Recollections of Three Reigns*. London: Eyre Methuen, 1951.

Pope-Hennessy, James. *Lord Crewe: The Likeness of a Liberal*. London: Constable, 1955.

————. *Queen Mary*. London: George Allen and Unwin, 1959.

"Power of the Royals, The," *The Guardian,* Jan. 9, 1995.

"Prince of Wales, The," *The Spectator,* Oct. 17, 1925.

Pryce-Jones, David. "TV Tale of Two Windsors," *The New York Times Magazine,* Mar. 18, 1979, p. 112.

Quennell, Peter, ed., James Pope-Hennessy, *A Lonely Business*. London: Weidenfeld and Nicolson, 1981.

Rocco, Fiametta. "A Strange Life: a profile of Prince Philip," *The Independent,* Dec. 13, 1992.

Romanones, Aline de, "The Dear Romance," *Vanity Fair,* June 1986.

Rose, Kenneth. *King George V.* London: Macmillan, 1983.

————. *Kings, Queen and Courtiers*. London: Weidenfeld and Nicolson, 1986.

Royal Family In Wartime, The. London: Odhams, 1945.

Ryan, Ann. "Prince Charles And The Ladies In Waiting," *Harper's Bazaar,* Oct. 1972.

St. Aubyn, Giles. *Edward VII*. London: Collins, 1979.

————. *Queen Victoria*. London: Sinclair-Stevenson, 1991.

Salway, Lance. *Queen Victoria's Grandchildren*. London: Collins and Brown, 1991.

Sarah, The Duchess of York, with Jeff Coplon. *My Story.* New York: Simon & Schuster, 1996.

BIBLIOGRAPHY

Seward, Ingrid. "Diana," *Majesty,* Oct. 1994.

———. *Diana: An Intimate Portrait.* Chicago: Contemporary Books, 1988.

———. *Royal Children.* London: HarperCollins, 1993.

———. *Sarah, HRH The Duchess of York.* London: Fontana/Harper-Collins, 1991.

Shew, Betty Spencer. *Queen Elizabeth, the Queen Mother.* London: Macdonald, 1955.

Shupbach, W. "The Last Moments of HRH The Prince Consort," *Medical History* 26 (1982).

Sinclair, David. *Two Georges: The Making of the Modern Monarchy.* London: Hodder & Stoughton, 1988.

Sinclair, Marianne, and Sarah Litvinoff, eds. *The Wit and Wisdom of the Royal Family: A Book of Quotes.* London: Plexus, 1990.

Small, Collie. "The Blooming of Margaret," *Collier's,* July 17, 1948.

Sondern, Frederic, Jr. "Royal Matriarch," *Life,* May 15, 1939.

Spink, Kathryn. *Invitation to a Royal Wedding.* New York: Crown, 1982.

Spoto, Donald. *The Decline and Fall of the House of Windsor.* New York: Simon & Schuster, 1995.

Stoeckl, Baroness Agnes de. *Not All Vanity.* London: John Murray, 1952.

Strachey, Lytton. *Queen Victoria.* London: Chatto & Windus, 1921.

Taylor, Noreen. "Saying What Everyone Thinks," *The Spectator,* Jan. 7, 1995.

Thornton, Michael. *Royal Feud.* London: Michael Joseph, 1985.

Tomlinson, Richard. *Divine Right: The Inglorious Survival of British Royalty.* London: Little, Brown, 1994.

Townsend, Peter. *Time and Chance*. London: Collins, 1978.

Trzebinski, Errol. *The Lives of Beryl Markham*. London: Heinemann, 1993.

Van der Kiste, John. *Edward VII's Children*. Phoenix Mill, England: Alan Sutton, 1989.

———. *George V's Children*. Phoenix Mill, England: Alan Sutton, 1991.

Vanderbilt, Gloria, and Thelma Lady Furness. *Double Exposure*. London: Frederick Muller, 1958.

Vansittart, Peter. *Happy and Glorious!* London: Collins, 1988.

Varney, Michael, with Max Marquis. *Bodyguard to Charles*. London: Robert Hale, 1989.

Vickers, Hugo. *Cecil Beaton*. London: Weidenfeld and Nicolson, 1986.

Walker, John. *The Queen Has Been Pleased: The Scandal of the British Honours System*. London: Sphere, 1986.

Wallace, Irving. "Princess Elizabeth," *Collier's*, Mar. 22, 1947.

Warwick, Christopher. *The Abdication*. London: Sidgwick & Jackson, 1986.

———. *George and Marina*. London: Weidenfeld and Nicolson, 1988.

Watson, Francis. "The Death of George V," *History Today*, Dec. 1986.

Weinreb, Ben, and Christopher Hibbert. *The London Encyclopedia*. London: Papermac/Macmillan, 1987.

Weintraub, Stanley. *Victoria*. New York: Dutton, 1988.

Weir, Alison. *Britain's Royal Families*. London: The Bodley Head, 1989.

Wheeler-Bennett, John. *King George VI: His Life and Reign*. London: Macmillan, 1958.

BIBLIOGRAPHY

Whitaker, James. *Diana v. Charles*. London: Signet, 1993.

Whiting, Audrey. *The Kents*. London: Futura, 1985.

Who's Who 1992. London: A & C Black, 1992.

Wilson, A. N. *The Rise and Fall of the House of Windsor*. London: Sinclair-Stevenson, 1993.

Wilson, Edgar. *The Myth of British Monarchy*. London: Journeyman/Republic, 1989.

Windsor, The Duchess of. *The Heart Has Its Reasons*. London: Michael Joseph, 1956.

Windsor, HRH The Duke of. *A Family Album*. London: Cassell, 1960.

————. *A King's Story*. London: Cassell, 1951.

Winter, Gordon, and Wendy Kochman. *Secrets of the Royals*. London: Robson, 1990.

Woman's Own, June 16, 1987.

Woodham-Smith, Cecil. *Queen Victoria: Her Life and Times*. London: Hamish Hamilton, 1972.

Woon, Basil. *The Real Sarah Bernhardt*. New York: Boni and Liveright, 1924.

Wrench, John Evelyn. *Geoffrey Dawson and Our Times*. London: Hutchinson, 1955.

Young, Kenneth, ed. *The Diaries of Sir Robert Bruce-Lockhart 1915–1938*. London: Macmillan, 1973.

Ziegler, Philip. *Diana Cooper*. London: Hamish Hamilton, 1981.

————. *King Edward VIII*. New York: Random House, 1991.

Videography and Discography

Diana, Princess of Wales: The BBC Recording of the Funeral Service. London Compact Disc 289 460 000-2, 1997.

Charles: A Man Alone. BBC-TV Video, 1994.

Charles and Diana: For Better or Worse. MPI Home Video 6185.

Charles: The Private Man, The Public Role, ITV documentary broadcast (United Kingdom), June 29, 1994.

Edward & Mrs. Simpson, a television drama with Edward Fox and Cynthia Harris. Thames Television/HBO Video 91070, 1991.

Elizabeth R. BBC Video 1001, 1992.

Elizabeth R: A Day in the Life. BBC Video, 1992.

Fergie: The Making of a Duchess. Independent Television News/Questar Video, 1990.

King's Story, A: The Love Story of the Century. International Historic Films 415, 1965.

Legacy of a Princess: The. Lifetime/ABC News MP 7275, 1996.

Monarchy, The. ITV (London Weekend), 1992.

Queen Elizabeth The Queen Mother: 90 Glorious Years. Public Media Video QUE 06 (BBC Enterprises), 1990.

Queen Elizabeth: The Power and the Glory. Questar Home Video, 1991.

VIDEOGRAPHY

Queen Is Crowned, A: The Coronation of HM Queen Elizabeth II. International Historic Films 369, 1985.

Queen Mother in Person, The. BBC-TV Video, 1993.

Queen's Birthday Parade, The. Public Media Video QUE 01, 1990.

Royal Family in Crisis, The. All American Television VHS, 1992.

Royal London. International Travel Films, 1991.

Royalty & Fashion: The Gowns & Jewels Worn by England's Royal Women. Questar Video, 1991.

Royalty: An Uncommon Working Family. International Historic Films 392, 1986.

Sarah Ferguson, Duchess of York. Prime Time Live (ABC-TV) Dec. 10, 1992.

Scandals of the Royal Family. Simitar VHS 2711, 1992.

Timewatch: The Prince of Wales. BBC-Z Channel, March 1994.

Touring Royal Castles and Stately Homes of England. Questar Video, 1992.

Windsors, The. A four-part ITV television series broadcast in the United Kingdom and the United States in 1994.

Index

INDEX

INDEX

Index

INDEX

About the Author

Donald Spoto is the author of fifteen books that have been translated into over twenty languages. Among the most famous are his biographies of Alfred Hitchcock, Tennessee Williams, Lotte Lenya, Laurence Olivier, Marlene Dietrich, Marilyn Monroe, Elizabeth Taylor, James Dean and *The Decline and Fall of the House of Windsor,* his history of the Royal Family from Victoria to Diana. His most recent book was *Notorious: The Life of Ingrid Bergman.*

Spoto's work has won him a listing in *Who's Who in America* and in *International Artists and Writers* for the last ten years, and he is the recipient of numerous awards in America and Europe—among them the Edgar for Best Nonfiction Book of the Year 1984, and Le Prix Star, France's highest award given to a writer, in 1993. His books regularly appear on best-seller lists in the United States and in many foreign countries.

Spoto earned his B.A. from Iona College and his M.A. and Ph.D. degrees from Fordham University, and for many years he taught on the university level in New York and California. Because of full-time literary commitments, he now restricts his lecturing to guest appearances, for which he is in demand worldwide. Recently, he has addressed audiences in London, Paris, Munich, Edinburgh, Chicago and Sydney, and in the autumn of 1996 he made his most recent appearances on numerous television programs in France, where he conducted all interviews in French. He lives in Beverly Hills, California. He is represented by Elaine Markson Literary Agency, New York.